Quadrille
PUBLISHING

Two
GREEDY
ITALIANS
eat
ITALY

Antonio CARLUCCIO *Gennaro* CONTALDO

PHOTOGRAPHY BY DAVID LOFTUS

Carluccio

My mother was very wise. She said that when God created Italy, He looked from a bird's eye view and found it was too beautiful. To provide a balancing element, He created the Italians! She also said that Jesus must have been Italian, firstly because He lived at home until the age of 33, secondly because He believed his mother to be a virgin, and thirdly, because the mother believed her son a god. Armed with these two gospels, I went out into the world to find out the truth. Over the years I discovered that Italians are by no means as perfect as I had thought, but I also recognised the one thing that unites all Italians: food, glorious food.

CONTALDO

We have been back to our beloved Italy, and indeed how beautiful it is – almost completely surrounded by sea, with its spectacular mountain ranges, valleys, lakes, rivers, plains and forests. How proud both of us feel to come from such a magnificent country! But, yes, then there are the Italians. As we discovered on our last trip home, many aspects of Italian life may be changing – with immigration, a breakdown of traditional family life, the fast-food culture – but the basic characteristics of the people themselves are still very much alive. Italians are different to other Europeans, in a multitude of ways, and we went on an exploratory journey, from north to south, to discover just why this is so...

Introduction

IT IS ONLY 150 YEARS SINCE ITALY BECAME A NATION. Until 1861, what is now Italy consisted of a number of separate city states or clearly defined regions, each with their own histories, their own cultures, customs and foods. Geography had played a major part in this: at one point the Alps formed a natural and impenetrable barrier between Italy and countries to the north while the Appenines – running along the length of the country like a backbone – prevented much communication between the regions in the west and east.

Geography still plays a paramount role in defining regional culinary styles, which is why we have divided the book into topographical chapters – dealing with the mountains and valleys, with the coastlines, and with the great plains and their rivers. So far as food is concerned – and we are, after all, greedy foodies – in the cooler north, the food eaten is generally attuned to climate (carbohydrate, meat, cheese), although it is almost impossible to generalise: there is a world of difference between what is eaten in the high mountains and in the great river cities of the plains. In the warmer south, where more exotic products are grown (tomatoes, aubergines, sweet peppers, kiwi fruit, citrus) the food is somehow lighter, sunnier and intenser. In the same way, geography can be said to define (and divide) the people too. The more industrial and, some say, industrious peoples of the north are cooler and more pragmatic than the hot-blooded, passionate inhabitants of the south.

Each region of what is now Italy, north and south, has at some point in the past been dominated or influenced by other civilisations or governing powers, and so a sense of 'Italian-ness' does not intrinsically exist. Instead Italians are by nature very loyal to family, to home, to friends, to locality – what is called '*campanalismo*', the pulling together of neighbours to defend their church bell-tower (*campanile*) from attack. It is no wonder then that Italians (with the example of recent governments in front of them) have a profound sense of the impermanence of anything remotely political and do not easily identify national interest with their own, being instead very adaptable in changing circumstances and good at solving problems. This is what is known as l'*arte di arrangiarsi*', the art of 'arranging oneself', or reaching into oneself, to do the best you possibly can with what you have. You can see this particularly in the harsh terrain of the northern Alps, where the people have to survive on very little, making the best of what they have – but it is equally apparent in the lives of those living in the poorer south, particularly those in Naples, where *arrangiarsi* is almost the supreme power…

Italians 'arrange' themselves so that they can feel good in themselves, and also to look good in the eyes of others. And this leads on to yet another Italian trait, the need to make a good impression in every single area of life. This is what is known as '*la bella figura*' (literally 'beautiful figure') that wanting to have and be the best – which we have seen historically, in art, design, architecture, music, fashion – and which applies, of course, to food too. Food is probably the most important thing in every Italian's life and, whatever else may be happening, meals must appear, the quality of the ingredients must be the best and the cooking must be superlative. Though such a trait seems admirable, *la bella figura* does have a negative side as well; it often borders on a bending of the truth, occasionally on superficiality, sometimes even on illegality.

On our travels we spent some time in Liguria, at the luxurious resort of Portofino, where the rich and famous moor their yachts and dine in the finest restaurants. There we saw how present-day *bella figura* influences people and food, but the glitz soon tarnished for us, and we couldn't wait to see – and eat – something real. The remainder of our time in Italy we spent in the south, in Rome and Lazio – exploring the capital city and its surroundings – and in Calabria, the toe of the Italian boot.

In a Lazio village, we encountered the machismo most often associated with Rome: in an eating contest, the winner must have eaten at least ten plates of pasta – and his size reflected this! In Rome itself, however, where they say all boys go to become men, big bellies were replaced with six-packs: *la bella figura* is obviously now as important as machismo. In Calabria, we were back in the beautiful land of our respective childhoods. Children are very much treasured in Italy – and they say that Italians in adulthood want to remain close, in some way, to that golden age when they were lovingly fed and pampered in every way. Our carefree childhoods were the best any child could wish for, and we wanted to see if this were still the case for southern children today. We were disturbed by the influx of American-type fast foods and snacks, which are contributing – in our beloved Italy! – to a rise in childhood obesity. But to our relief, the love and wonderful food are still there.

Carluccio

My mother would be astounded at some of the changes that have become apparent in Italian society, culture and food. However, she would still recognise her fellow Italians – some essential traits never change! – and that all-embracing love of life, food and children that so characterises the typical Italian would be very familiar to her. It was wonderful to be back in Italy, both working on the book and on the television series. As usual, Gennaro and I had our moments. We laughed, we fought, we tasted, we cooked. We met some incredible people, went to some extraordinary places, travelled from north to south, from mountain to plain, lake to sea, in fast cars and camper vans, and we ate an astonishing variety of foods. Italy may have changed in many ways since we were boys (a long time ago), but at heart she is still our much loved bella Italia.

CONTALDO

It has been another interesting journey rediscovering our bella Italia and spending time together again. We have especially enjoyed reflecting upon all those typical Italian characteristics, which we now look on as outsiders, as neither of us has lived in Italy for over 30 years. But we can also identify ourselves with them. I thought I had lost these traits, but Antonio says I am the definition of l'arte di arrangiarsi and la bella figura – and so is he! We both like to be seen as macho, but have to admit that we were only too happy to run to the safe haven of our mother's home even as young adults. We hope you will join us on this new journey throughout Italy, and enjoy recreating the recipes which reflect the diverse geography and culture of a much loved nation.

COMFORT FOOD
from the mountains

ITALY IS ALMOST ENTIRELY COVERED WITH MOUNTAINS. The two main ranges are the Alps and the Appenines. The Alps, which include the Dolomites, run from west to east across northern Italy, bordering with France, Switzerland and Austria. The Appenines stretch from Liguria in the north to the very south, forming the backbone of Italy. Mountains are formed by volcanic action, and Italy is still volcanically active: she has Vesuvius (the only active volcano on the European mainland), Etna (on Sicily) and Stromboli (on the island of the same name). Interestingly, the ash and other deposits from volcanic eruptions in time contribute to a very rich soil, perfect for agriculture.

With mountains come valleys, mountain lakes and mountain weather. Life in the harsh winter conditions of the Alpine valleys for early settlers was hazardous and isolationist: traditions were handed down from generation to generation with little influence from the outside world. It is not uncommon, even today, for Italians from other regions to call people from the mountains, slightly mockingly, '*i montanari*'. Communication between different countries, regions and even valleys was always difficult, but then roads were built, then tunnels, then railway lines (often under the mountains). Today the mountains of the Alps are chic ski resorts during winter; in summer, they are a paradise for walkers wanting to savour the peace and pure fresh air.

Carluccio

The Appenines touch almost every region of Italy from north to south. These mountains form one of the most complex reservoirs of flora, fauna and waterways, all of which supply their own people and those of the coastal areas with the highest-quality ingredients for producing wonderful food.

Mountain food, especially in the north, has traditionally been calorific, rich in carbohydrates and proteins to withstand the cold of winter. Although wheat and maize are mostly grown in the plains and in the fertile pre-Alps, dried pasta and polenta are the primary carbohydrates. The hardy buckwheat can be grown at considerable altitude – and is used in the Valtellina to make *pizzoccheri*. Not much can be reliably grown, so the local people have to make the best of what they have, or what they can acquire through foraging or hunting.

In the high Alpine valleys are rich pastures of grasses, wild herbs and flowers, and this is where the cows are taken in spring and summer. As a result wonderful cow's milk cheeses – Fontina, Taleggio, Asiago and Gorgonzola among them – are produced. Because of the ready availability of cow's milk, butter and cream are normally used in northern cooking, replacing the olive oil used in the rest of Italy.

Carbohydrate and protein are mixed in steaming bowls of polenta enriched with butter and cheese: served with a robust *spezzatino* (stew) of meat or game (hunting is a passion here), this is a popular meal for most families. In the Aosta Valley bordering France, Fontina cheese features heavily in local dishes like *fonduta* (the Italian version of fondue). Far from the sea, many Alpine regions rely on preserved fish for additional protein and flavour (anchovies in *bagna cauda*, for instance). Vegetables are preserved too – vital for survival throughout the winter – as are meats: pigs are bred in the mountains and are made into salami and hams, the latter hanging in special barns high in the Alps to take advantage of the plentiful, pure and drying air. Bresaola is a cured beef which is air-dried in the Valtellina; very similar to the *Bündnerfleisch* of nearby Switzerland. It sells well, primarily because it is able to be enjoyed by those unable to eat pork.

One interesting aspect of Alpine food is the influence other countries' cuisines have had on it. In Trentino-Alto Adige to the east, there are distinct Germanic influences: sauerkraut is common, as are *canederli* or *Knödeln* (two types of bread dumpling). Elsewhere there are French, Austrian, Swiss, Yugoslavian, even Hungarian influences, reflecting a shared topography, ingredients, and perhaps, at some point in the past, shared government.

The mountains and valleys of Italy are carpeted with forests and woods. The lower levels of the Alps are home to beech, oak and chestnut trees. Chestnuts, once food for the poor, are now a delicacy in local restaurants. A large variety of mushrooms can be found in autumn, when groups of people can be seen foraging for porcini, chanterelles, and other edible species. (Truffles are a different matter.) Olive trees are also grown in the north on the lower slopes of mountains, and in rocky Liguria they are grown in terraces so inaccessible the fruit has to be picked by hand. No land is ever wasted (vegetables are often grown between trees) and olive trees in Tuscany, Puglia and Calabria clothe the most unlikely of slopes, as do acres of grape vines, planted on the side of the valley that will get most sun.

Further south, along the length of the Appenines where the weather is warmer and pastures are not so lush, it is goats and sheep that dominate the valleys, producing some excellent local cheeses including the famous pecorino. Meat dishes of lamb, sheep and goat are popular and eaten traditionally at festive times, like *abbacchio* (baby lamb) at Easter. Temperate fruit and nut trees are grown at heights and temperatures at which you think they could not thrive – but thrive they do – and some of the best Italian fruit come from the foothills of Campania.

Mountain food is honest food. It may lack the excitement of dishes of other areas of Italy, but it is extremely tasty and wholesome.

1 litre strong **beef stock** or
  broth (you could use
  Gennaro's, see page 16)
500ml **white wine**
4 slices good country **bread**
40g **unsalted butter**
½ tsp **ground cinnamon**
100ml **double cream**
100g **Parmesan**, freshly grated,
  plus extra to serve

SERVES 4

Carluccio

Eisacktaler Weinsuppe
BEEF AND WINE SOUP

From Eisacktaler in the Italian Valle d'Isarco – the extreme eastern part of the Alps – comes this heart-warming and delightful soup. There as many people speak German as they do Italian, thus the name 'wine soup', a good example of the influence neighbouring countries have on the Italian regions and their food.

Put the stock and the wine together in a large saucepan, bring to the boil and cook for 1 minute only. Remove from the heat and set aside.

Fry the bread in the butter on both sides until golden, then sprinkle with the cinnamon. Put a slice in each soup bowl.

Add the cream to the soup, and heat gently to warm through. Stir in the Parmesan. Pour over the bread in the bowls, and sprinkle with a little more Parmesan before serving.

BEEF BROTH

1kg **beef brisket**

2 large **onions**, cut into chunks

2 **celery stalks**, cut into chunks
and the leaves

2 large **carrots**, cut into chunks

6 **bay leaves**

24 **black peppercorns**

salt

2.4 litres **water**

CANEDERLI

200g stale **bread**, cubed

200ml **milk**, warmed

butter, for frying

½ **onion**, very finely chopped

1 tbsp chopped **parsley**

20g **plain flour**, plus extra for
dusting

40g **speck** or **prosciutto**, very
finely chopped

1 **egg**, beaten

20g **Parmesan**, freshly grated

salt

1 tbsp chopped **chives**, to garnish

SERVES 4

Canederli in Brodo di Manzo
BREAD DUMPLINGS IN BEEF BROTH

These bread dumplings are a speciality of the mountainous Trentino-Alto Adige region. Legend says canederli *were invented by a housewife ordered to feed a group of soldiers: she did not hesitate, and immediately gathered together her leftovers. Whatever their origin, these hearty bread dumplings are ideal nutrition for this mountainous region and can be eaten in a broth or with a stew. Here I have combined them with a home-made beef broth, the perfect filling dish for cold winter evenings. While I certainly wouldn't follow them with another course, you could always have the beef and vegetables from the broth afterwards as a main.*

First make the beef broth. Place all the ingredients into a large pot, bring to the boil and gently simmer for about 3–4 hours, skimming off the fat from the surface if necessary, until the meat is tender and falling apart. Remove the meat and vegetables from the stock and use another time. Strain the liquid and set aside in a saucepan.

To make the *canederli*, place the bread in a large bowl, pour over the milk and leave to absorb. Melt the butter in a small pan, add the onion and sweat until softened. Add to the bread along with the rest of the ingredients except the chives. Combine well and leave to rest for about 15 minutes before shaping into walnut-sized balls. Dust some flour on a plate or tray and place the *canederli* on it to avoid sticking.

Warm the broth. Bring a large saucepan of slightly salted water to the boil, drop in the *canederli* and cook for 15 minutes on a medium to high heat. Lift gently with a slotted spoon, divide between 4 individual bowls and serve with a couple of ladles of hot beef broth. Garnish with chopped chives.

Carluccio

Schwammersuppe
CHANTERELLE SOUP

Wild mushrooms play an important part in the gastronomy of Italy, particularly in the Alps – where masses of fungi grow and are collected on the wooded slopes of the lower mountains and hills.

Chop most of the fresh chanterelles, keeping a few whole for garnish.

To make the soup base, melt 50g of the butter in a large saucepan, then add the flour and cook, stirring continuously, until the flour starts to change colour. Gradually add the chicken stock, a little at a time, continuing to stir to avoid lumps. Keep warm over a gentle heat.

Melt the remaining butter in another large saucepan, and fry the onion and garlic until softened. Add all the chanterelles and fry for 6–7 minutes. Add the chopped parsley and some salt to taste. Take out the whole chanterelles and set aside. Tip everything else into the soup-base liquid, and stir well. Taste and adjust the seasoning, then stir in the cream. Serve in warm bowls, topped with the whole mushrooms and accompanied by lightly toasted crusty bread.

250g fresh **chanterelles**, cleaned
90g **unsalted butter**
60g **plain flour**
1.5 litres **chicken stock**
1 small **onion**, very finely chopped
1 **garlic clove**, finely chopped
1 tbsp finely chopped **flat-leaf parsley**
salt and freshly ground **black pepper**
4 tbsp **double cream**

SERVES 4

mixed raw vegetables, such
    as celery, carrots, peppers,
    asparagus, fennel, spring
    onions, Jerusalem artichokes,
    celeriac, radishes, beetroot

DIP
enough **milk** to cover the garlic
8 **garlic cloves,** cut into thin slices
12 **anchovy fillets**
70g **unsalted butter**
150ml **olive oil**
100ml **double cream**

SERVES 6–8

Carluccio

Bagna Cauda
ANCHOVY AND GARLIC DIP

A hot dip for raw vegetables, this is eaten mostly in Piedmont and the Aosta Valley (both areas far from the sea, but which are passionate about anchovies). Many would say it is an anti-social dish because of the garlic, but this version is exceptionally tasty and without any side-effects. Indeed, I would say it is the opposite – it is best eaten with everyone sitting around a table, all dipping their tender vegetables into the same pot of warm sauce on a burner in the middle.

First prepare the vegetables (you could just offer two or three) by cutting them into strips, sticks or slices.

In a fondue pot or similar, heat the milk and the garlic gently for about 15 minutes, or until the garlic is soft. Remove from the heat, and add the anchovies. Stir to dissolve the fish into the milk. Add the butter, oil and cream.

Gently warm the sauce through and keep it warm throughout the dipping process above a nightlight or low flame. Serve with some good country bread cut into soldiers.

400g fresh **porcini** (cep)
50g **breadcrumbs**
2 tbsp **plain flour**
1 tsp chopped **thyme**
2 **eggs**, beaten
50ml **milk**
freshly ground **black pepper**
olive oil, for frying

SERVES 4

CONTALDO

Funghi Impanati e Fritti
BREADCRUMBED AND FRIED PORCINI MUSHROOMS

Porcini (ceps) and other wild fungi are much sought after in the woods and valleys of Italy's mountains. This is a simple recipe which maximises their flavour. If you can't get hold of porcini, use the large portobello mushroom that is widely available. Serve with a few salad leaves and/or preserved vegetables.

Clean the mushrooms with a damp cloth and slice lengthways. Combine the breadcrumbs, flour and thyme in a dish. In a bowl, combine the beaten egg, milk and pepper. Dip the porcini slices in the egg, then coat with the breadcrumb mixture.

Heat an abundant amount of oil in a pan and fry the mushrooms a few at a time until golden. Drain well. Serve with a sprinkle of freshly ground black pepper. These mushrooms are delicious hot but can also be eaten cold.

The Lakes

OF THE MANY LAKES THROUGHOUT ITALY, IT IS THE STRING OF NARROW GLACIAL LAKES IN THE NORTH WHICH ARE THE BEST KNOWN – Como, Maggiore, Garda and Lugano (the latter part Italian, part Swiss). Surrounded by the snow-covered Alps, their beautiful scenery and pure air have been popular since Roman times.

Lake Garda, the largest in Italy, is divided between three regions: Veneto, Lombardy and Trentino. The lake acts like a huge solar panel and the mountains as an insulator keeping the heat in. As a result, the olive and vine groves on the banks produce excellent olive oil, wine and even lemons, which are used to make a local liqueur, limoncino. Lake Maggiore, the second largest, borders with Switzerland in the north. The upper end of the lake is completely alpine, the middle part hilly and the lower end advances towards the plains of Lombardy. As with Lake Garda, the mountains surrounding the lake protect and insulate, making for a mild climate all year round.

With such a diverse landscape, the food of these two lakes is eclectic. The valleys have a history of high-quality cheese making; local delicacies include *Bettelmatt* and *Ossolano d'Alpe*. Cheese is also made on the shores, such as the goat's cheese, *formagella*. These areas also produce excellent honey and fantastic cured meats including *mortadella d'Ossola* (recognised by the Slow Food movement), *violini di capra* (cured goat's leg), various salami and the renowned cured beef, bresaola.

Lake Como, shaped like an upside down Y, is Italy's third largest lake and the deepest in Europe. Situated in Lombardy at the foot of the Alps, it has always been a popular retreat for the wealthy. Its palatial lakeside villas have been turned into luxurious hotels, and many are second homes for rich Milanese as well as some Hollywood celebrities!

The food around Como is typical of the Lombardy region. Polenta has always been a staple, served with meat and game dishes. Typical dishes of risotto, *cotoletta*, *ossobuco* and *pizzoccheri* can be found in local restaurants and desserts feature *cutiza* (apple fritters) and *resca de comm*, a type of doughy cake with dried fruit and nuts.

All the lakes have an abundance of fish and varieties include pike, tench, eel, carp and trout. There is a local tradition of preserving fish and a lot of the regional recipes include *carpione* (fish preserved by cooking, then marinating), and *missoltit* (*agone* fish sun-dried on the shores of Lake Como).

Towards central Italy is the next largest lake, Trasimeno in Umbria.
It does not have the grandeur of the northern lakes but its proximity to
tourist destinations such as Perugia, Florence and Siena makes it popular.
The high hills on the eastern side partially protect it from cold winds, and the
climate is quite mild with humid summers. The hills are rich in olive and vine
groves and the western shores are occupied by fruit and vegetable plantations.
The area boasts fine wines, the Umbrian truffle and wild boar sausages. Fish
is used in specialities like *tegamaccio*, a fish stew, and carp cooked over a
wooden fire.

Near Rome are the smaller, hardly known volcanic lakes of Lazio, offering
peace from the bustling capital. The larger lakes of Bolsena and Bracciano
claim to be the cleanest in Italy: motorboats are prohibited except for
authorised fishermen. Lake Bracciano also provides much of Rome with its
drinking water. The surrounding countryside is dominated by olive groves
and orange trees. As well as fish from the lakes – perch, whitefish, eel – the
cuisine is heavily influenced by products of the land: meat such as baby
lamb (*abbacchio*), baby pig (*porchetta*), oxtail and tripe, as well as the famous
pecorino romano and *caciotta* cheeses and an array of vegetables.

CONTALDO

400g **Fontina cheese**
300ml **milk**
4 **egg yolks**
30g **unsalted butter**
salt and freshly ground **black pepper**
1 **black** or **white truffle**, thinly sliced (optional)

SERVES 4–6

Carluccio

Fonduta Valdostana con Tartufo
FONDUE WITH FONTINA CHEESE AND TRUFFLE

Fonduta is a dialect word for 'melted'. Though this recipe may have been influenced by the cheese fondue of the Swiss on the other side of the border, the people of the Aosta Valley and Piedmontese in general say it is entirely Italian. It is made in a different way to the Swiss version, but the principle is the same – you dip bread into a warm, cheesy cream. Heavenly…This fonduta mixture is also very good served on roasted peppers, or as a stuffing for choux pastry puffs or eclairs, or puff pastry vol-au-vents.

Cut the Fontina into small cubes, put into a bowl, and cover with the milk. Leave to marinate for 3–4 hours.

Put the milk and cheese into a suitable pan and melt the cheese very, very gently until the mixture is creamy in consistency. Stir in the egg yolks one by one. Add the butter and season to taste.

Pour the *fonduta* into a large fondue or similar pot and place over nightlights or a low flame. Serve with slices of truffle. Eat the *fonduta* by dipping slices of toasted country bread into the cheese mixture.

Carluccio

Aringhe alla Casalinga
CURED HERRING WITH APPLES

This antipasto – which could also be a main course – comes from the north-east German-speaking corner of Italy, the Südtirol or Alto Adige, where the Austrian influences are still felt. For it you need cured herring, not rollmops. Matjes herring are caught when very fat, marinated in a salt brine for a year, then filleted and kept in oil. They are a great delicacy.

Cook the potatoes in lightly salted water until tender. Drain, leave to cool and remove the skins.

Arrange the herring fillets on a serving platter and cover with the sliced onion and apple. Pour the cream over the top and serve with the boiled potatoes. Occasionally this dish is accompanied by a small glass of Schnapps, a dry liqueur tasting of plums.

8 **new potatoes**
salt
8 **matjes herring fillets** in oil
1 small **onion**, finely sliced
1 **apple**, peeled, cored and finely sliced
125ml **double cream**

SERVES 4

Preserved Fish *Carluccio*

Over the centuries, preserved fish have been extremely important to the Italian diet. The anchovy is probably the most significant: caught in the south, it is salted, canned, brined, made into an essence (*colatura*), bottled as sauce, and used in numerous dishes to add flavour and kick.

Baccalà and *stocco*, salted and air-dried cod, are a curiosity; although small cod are found in Italian waters and used fresh, the preserved fish have been imported for centuries. Herring are another northern fish, but much loved when salt-cured and smoked. Thin slices of salted, air-dried tuna, *mosciame* (sometimes swordfish as well), make a delicious, if expensive, antipasto; and *bottarga*, the cured roe of grey mullet and tuna, can be grated on pasta, rice or eggs to impart a delicate fishy flavour, or eaten in slices.

3 slices of **bread**
2 tbsp **extra virgin olive oil**
2 **gem lettuce**, leaves separated
a small handful of **wild rocket**
100g **radishes**, sliced
20 **black olives**
2 **eggs**, hard-boiled and quartered
80g **bresaola**, thinly sliced
2 tbsp finely shaved fresh
   Parmesan

DRESSING
4 tbsp **extra virgin olive oil**
2 tbsp **white wine vinegar**
salt and freshly ground **black**
   pepper
1 **garlic clove**, left whole and
   pierced with a knife

SERVES 4

CONTALDO

Insalata della Valtellina

BRESAOLA SALAD

This simple but nutritious salad is satisfying enough to have as a main course. Bresaola is cured, air-dried beef typically made in the Valtellina area of Lombardy. Lean and tender and with little added salt it is perfect in salads, and is readily available in Italian delis and larger supermarkets.

Remove the crusts from the bread and slice into small triangles. Heat the oil in a frying pan, add the bread and fry on both sides until golden. Remove and leave to dry on kitchen paper.

Meanwhile make the dressing. Combine all the dressing ingredients and whisk together with a fork until you obtain a creamy consistency. Remove the garlic clove from the dressing.

Arrange the lettuce leaves, rocket, radishes and olives on a serving dish, pour over the dressing and toss well. Arrange the eggs, bresaola and fried bread and scatter over the Parmesan shavings.

Cured Meats *Carluccio*

The pig reigns supreme in the cured meat world, most famously as Parma ham (*prosciutto crudo*), the hind leg of pig which is cured and dried for at least 18 months. Pancetta is cured bacon belly and is often smoked. *Guanciale* is cured pig cheek, the authentic bacon to use in many pasta sauces. Speck is a smoked, salt-cured, air-dried ham, made from the shoulder. Then there are the endless varieties of salami and bresaola, a cured air-dried beef. All these can be sliced for antipasto, or used in cooking.

Carluccio

Pizzoccheri
BUCKWHEAT PASTA WITH POTATOES AND SWISS CHARD

This is proper comfort food, a prime example of l'arte di arrangiarsi *– the art of making the best of what you have. Created in the Valtellina, one of the valleys of Lombardy just north of Milan, it uses simple local produce: pasta made from* grano saraceno, *or buckwheat, Bitto cheese, wonderful butter and many vegetables. The pasta itself – a sort of large tagliatelle – used to be made by hand, but it is now possible to buy it dried in packets in good delicatessens.*

Preheat the oven to 220°C/Gas 7.

Put the *pizzoccheri,* potatoes and Swiss chard in a large saucepan and cover with lightly salted boiling water. Cook together until soft, about 14 minutes.

Meanwhile, melt the butter in a small frying pan and fry the garlic until cooked but not brown.

Drain the pasta, potatoes and chard and put in a large ovenproof dish. While still warm, mix in the cubes of cheese. Pour over the foaming butter and garlic and sprinkle over the Parmesan. Season to taste with salt and pepper, then mix together well.

Bake in the hot oven for 20 minutes. Serve hot.

300g *pizzoccheri* (made usually with ⅓ Italian '00' flour, ⅔ buckwheat flour)
200g waxy **potatoes**, peeled and cut into small cubes
200g **Swiss chard**, leaves only
salt and freshly ground **black pepper**
80g **unsalted butter**
3 **garlic cloves**, sliced
300g **Bitto** or **Toma cheese**, cut into small cubes
100g **Parmesan**, freshly grated

SERVES 4–6

400g **porcini** (cep)
4 tbsp **extra virgin olive oil**
1 **shallot**, finely chopped
1 **garlic clove**, finely chopped
salt and freshly ground **black
  pepper**
300ml **double cream**
3 sprigs of **thyme**
120g **speck,** or prosciutto
  thinly sliced
350g *pappardelle*
50g **Parmesan**, freshly grated

SERVES 4

CONTALDO

Pappardelle con Speck e Porcini

PAPPARDELLE WITH SPECK AND PORCINI

As a rule I don't like to use cream in my cooking, but when I tested this recipe for this book, I have to admit I began to change my opinion! The combination of porcini, speck, thyme and cream is truly delicious: even my daughter, who is a fussy eater, cleaned her plate. Speck is a cured pork meat originating from the Südtirol, or Alto Adige, which once belonged to Austria and is now part of Italy. Similar in appearance to prosciutto, with a slight smoky taste, it is only in recent years that it has been introduced to the rest of Italy and can now be bought in good Italian delis.

Clean the mushrooms with a damp cloth and thinly slice. Heat the oil in a frying pan, add the mushrooms and sauté for a few minutes until golden. Add the shallot and garlic and sauté for a minute. Season with salt and pepper. Stir in the cream and thyme, lower the heat, add the speck and cook until the cream thickens slightly.

In the meantime, cook the pasta in plenty of slightly salted water until *al dente*, drain and add to the sauce. Add the Parmesan, mix well, remove from the heat and serve immediately.

1.5 litres **chicken or vegetable stock**

400g **mixed wild mushroom**s such as fresh or dried porcini (ceps), chanterelles, horn of plenty, birch boletes

1 small **onion**, finely chopped

3 tbsp **olive oil**

100g **unsalted butter**

350g **carnaroli risotto rice**

salt and freshly ground **black pepper**

60g **Parmesan**, finely grated

SERVES 4

Carluccio

Risotto con Funghi Misti
RISOTTO WITH MIXED MUSHROOMS

They say that a risotto made with just porcini represents the height of gustatory pleasure (only beaten by one served with truffles). But the satisfaction of coming back from a fungi hunt in the woods and mountains with lots of different mushrooms, with their many colours, textures and tastes, can be just as exhilarating.

Put the stock in a saucepan and bring to a gentle simmer. Leave over a low heat.

Gently clean the porcini and other mushrooms, using a sharp knife and a brush (avoid washing them whenever possible). If you are using dried porcini, put them to soak in a small bowl of water for 15 minutes. Slice the fresh mushrooms, putting a few good slices aside for decoration.

Fry the onion in the oil and half of the butter. When the onion begins to colour, add the sliced mushrooms and continue to fry over a moderate flame for a couple of minutes. If using dried porcini, chop them into small pieces and add to the mushrooms, keeping the water they soaked in to add to the risotto later with the stock.

Add the rice and stir for a minute, until all the grains are coated in the fat. Start to add the hot stock, ladle by ladle. Wait until each ladleful is absorbed before adding the next. Add the porcini soaking water if you have it. When the rice is *al dente*, remove from the heat, season and stir in the remaining butter and the Parmesan cheese. Serve hot, decorating each portion with a slice or two of raw mushroom.

500g strong **plain flour**, plus extra for dusting

2 tsp **salt**

1 x 7g sachet of **dried yeast**

320ml lukewarm **water**

a few **dried breadcrumbs** or a bit of semolina, for dusting

TOPPING

80g **Gruyère cheese**, grated

250g **crème fraîche**

salt and freshly ground **black pepper**

1 large **red onion**, thinly sliced

140g **salami**, cut into strips

a few **marjoram leaves**

MAKES 2 LARGE PIZZAS

Torta Salata delle Alpi
ALPINE PIZZA

Although pizza was born in Naples, it is of course now eaten all over Italy – and the world. I am so used to topping it with the usual tomato, mozzarella, basil, anchovies and olives, but this more robust alternative is a most pleasant surprise. Although Gruyère is not an Italian cheese, it goes really well with this 'pizza of the mountains', and is readily available to buy. Be warned, this is a very filling pizza, but it's also very delicious!

Preheat the oven to 240°C/Gas 9. Combine the flour, salt and yeast in a large bowl. Gradually add the water, mixing well with your hands to obtain a dough. If you find the dough too sticky, simply add a little more flour. Shape into a ball, cover with a cloth and leave to rest for 5 minutes. Knead the dough for about 10 minutes and split it in half. Sprinkle some flour on a clean kitchen cloth and place the pieces of dough on it. Cover with a slightly damp cloth and leave to rise for at least 30 minutes in a warm place.

Meanwhile combine the Gruyère and crème fraîche in a bowl, adding some salt and pepper to taste. Set aside.

Sprinkle some flour on a clean work surface and spread the dough into a circle about 30cm in diameter, making it as thin as possible (without tearing it), with the border slightly thicker. Repeat with the other dough ball. Sprinkle two flat baking trays with breadcrumbs or semolina and place the pizza bases on them.

Spread the crème fraîche mixture over each base. Top with the onions and salami. Bake in the hot oven for 10 minutes. Remove, sprinkle with the marjoram and serve.

Polenta e Fagioli Borlotti al Forno

POLENTA AND BORLOTTI BEAN BAKE

Maize for polenta is grown in the Po Delta and in the pre-Alps, as well as further south. The tradition of combining polenta with beans is of Tuscan origin, although a similar version is found in the mountainous area around Parma. Filling and substantial, this is a real 'slow food' dish to be savoured on winter evenings.

200g dried **borlotti beans**
5 tbsp **extra virgin olive oil**, plus extra for drizzling
1 small **onion**, finely chopped
1 **celery stalk**, finely chopped
1 **leek**, finely chopped
1 large **carrot**, finely chopped
80g **pancetta**, roughly chopped
10 **cherry tomatoes**, halved
100g **quick-cook polenta**
a handful of **parsley**, finely chopped
80g **Fontina cheese**, cubed
salt

SERVES 6

Place the beans in plenty of cold water and leave to soak overnight. The next day, drain and cook in plenty of fresh water for about 40 minutes until tender (check the packet instructions for details as timings may vary). Drain and set aside.

Heat the oil in a pan, add the onions, celery, leeks and carrot and fry for a couple of minutes, stirring. Add the pancetta and continue to cook, stirring, for a minute. Add the cherry tomatoes and cooked borlotti beans. Remove from the heat and set aside.

Preheat the oven to 200°C/Gas 6. Make up the polenta according to the instructions on the packet. Have some boiling water ready to add if you need extra and keep stirring with a wooden spoon to prevent lumps from forming. Remove from the heat, stir in the parsley and the Fontina cheese and season with salt to taste. Carefully add about three-quarters of the bean mixture until all combined.

Grease the bottom of a terracotta or ovenproof dish with some butter. Pour the polenta mixture into it, topping with the remaining beans. Cook in the preheated oven for about 15 minutes until golden. Remove and serve.

Beans and Pulses
Carluccio

Dried beans and pulses were once the food of the poor and unfashionable, but traditional dishes have recently become popular again. Before the discovery of the New World the broad bean was once the only bean eaten in Italy, but now there is a large variety. Tuscan broad beans are eaten fresh and raw with pecorino. Borlotti, with their multicoloured pods and beans, and cannellini, which are creamy white in colour, can both be eaten fresh or dried, in soups or salads. Lentils and chickpeas are used in many ways, stewed, puréed and added to soups. Chickpeas can also be ground to flour and used to make Ligurian flatbread and fritters.

500g **potatoes**
250g **chestnut flour**
50g **plain flour**
1 tsp **salt**
2 **eggs**
rice flour, for dusting

SAUCE
100g **butter**
6 **sage leaves**
20g **Parmesan**, freshly grated

SERVES 4

Gnocchi di Castagne con Burro e Salvia
CHESTNUT GNOCCHI WITH A BUTTER AND SAGE SAUCE

Chestnut trees are a common sight all over northern Italy, and in autumn chestnut-collecting is a popular pastime. Chestnuts were commonly consumed throughout Italy in the days when poor people had little to eat, because they were free and rich in carbohydrate. Chestnut flour was once made into a form of polenta, and can also sometimes be used to make pasta and gnocchi. It is the basis of the famous castagnaccio *cake, and is found in a variety of breads and desserts. Here, the chestnut adds a slightly sweet flavour to the gnocchi and marries extremely well with the butter and sage sauce. Chestnut flour can be obtained from good delis.*

Boil the potatoes, drain and mash them. Place in a large bowl and combine with the chestnut flour, plain flour and salt. Add the eggs and mix well to make a dough. Sprinkle some rice flour on a work surface and roll out the dough into long sausage shapes. With a sharp knife, cut out squares of approximately 2cm. Press the tines of a fork into the squares to create ridges.

Place a large saucepan of slightly salted water on the heat and bring to the boil. At the same time, melt the butter in a large frying pan together with the sage leaves. When the water boils, drop in the gnocchi and cook until they come up to the surface. Lift out with a slotted spoon and add to the butter and sage sauce together with a little of the cooking water. Mix well, remove from the heat and sprinkle with Parmesan. Serve immediately.

1kg **topside of beef**
1 **garlic clove**
2 **bay leaves**
2 sprigs of **rosemary**
8 black **peppercorns**
1 large **onion**, finely chopped
3 **carrots**, finely chopped
2 **celery stalks**, finely chopped
1 bottle of **red wine**
6 tbsp **extra virgin olive oil**
salt

SERVES 4

Brasato di Manzo in Vino Rosso
BRAISED BEEF IN RED WINE

This is a typically robust Piedmontese dish which is normally cooked with Barolo wine from the area. Marinating the beef with the vegetables, herbs and wine gives the best flavour, but if you are pressed for time, you can omit this stage. Traditionally served with steaming polenta (see page 39), this hearty winter dish is equally good with mashed potato.

Pat the meat all over gently with kitchen paper to dry. Place in a large bowl together with all the other ingredients except for the oil and salt. Cover with clingfilm and marinate in the fridge overnight, or for at least 12 hours.

Remove the meat from the marinade and pat dry with kitchen paper. Heat the oil in a large saucepan, add the meat and seal well all over. Remove and set aside.

In the same saucepan, add the vegetables and herbs from the marinade and sweat for a couple of minutes. Return the meat to the pan, add some salt and cook on a medium heat for 10 minutes. Add the wine from the marinade, bring to the boil, then reduce the heat to low and cover with a lid. Cook for about 2 hours, until the meat is tender and the liquid has reduced, checking from time to time and gently turning over during cooking. Check for seasoning. Remove the meat, slice and place on a serving dish together with the vegetables and sauce.

2 **pheasants** (or wild rabbit),
   about 800g–1kg,
   cleaned and cut into chunks
plain flour, for coating
salt and freshly ground **black
   pepper**
olive oil, for frying
1 **celery stalk**, cut into small
   cubes
1 **carrot**, cut into small cubes
1 small **onion**, finely sliced
50g **speck**, roughly chopped
40g dried **porcini** (ceps), soaked
   for 30 minutes then drained
   and finely chopped
100ml **red wine**
a pinch of freshly grated **nutmeg**
a pinch of **powdered cinnamon**
1 tbsp **tomato purée** diluted in
   150ml water
400g **carnaroli risotto rice**
1.5 litres **water**
50g **unsalted butter**
50g **Parmesan**, freshly grated

SERVES 4–6

Carluccio

Ragù di Fagiano con Corona di Riso

PHEASANT STEW WITH A CROWN OF RICE

In the mountains throughout Italy many types of game are shot and cooked in a variety of ways. Pheasant is popular in the north and centre of Italy, especially in the Tuscan and Umbrian Appenines, and is usually just roasted: this is the only pheasant stew that I am aware of. There are dried porcini (ceps) in the sauce, and a crown of flavourful rice accompanies it wonderfully. I have also made this stew with wild rabbit, which was exceptional.

Coat the pieces of pheasant in flour, shaking off any excess, and season with salt and pepper. Heat 4–6 tablespoons of oil in a large frying pan, add the pieces and fry on each side until brown, about 6–8 minutes. Remove from the pan and set aside.

In the same pan, perhaps with another 2–3 tablespoons of oil, fry the celery, carrot, onion and speck to soften them, about 10 minutes. Add the porcini, stirring, then pour in the wine and cook for 5 minutes. Add some salt, pepper, nutmeg, cinnamon and the tomato purée and water. Put the pheasant pieces back into the sauce, cover with the lid and cook slowly for an hour, or until the pheasant is tender. Check from time to time, adding a little extra water if required.

Cook the rice in lightly salted boiling water for 16 minutes or until all the water has been absorbed. Stir in the butter and Parmesan.

Arrange the rice in a circle around the edges of a serving platter, place the pheasant ragù in the middle, and serve.

Cervo alla Tirolese

VENISON STEW

Italians are very trigger happy in general, with a lust for hunting and a tendency to shoot at anything that moves – which can have painful consequences when, occasionally, some hunters become the hunted! The comoscio, or wild goat, lives in the very high mountains in the Alps, towards the eastern borders with Austria and Croatia. The locals are allowed to cull some of these goats to help balance the population, which they often make into a stew. As wild goat can be difficult to get hold of in the local supermarket, I've used venison here instead.

Put the venison and all the ingredients for the marinade into a pot large enough to hold the meat snugly. The marinade should cover the meat. Leave to marinate for 24 hours.

Remove the meat and the vegetables from the marinade. Set the meat to one side, reserve the marinade and muslin bag. Wash out the pot. Chop the vegetables.

Heat the oil in the same pot, and fry the speck and porcini, then the carrot, celery and onion, until all are soft, about 7–8 minutes. Add the meat, then the wine and muslin bag, and stir in the tomato paste and water. Season with salt and pepper, cover the pot, and cook over a low heat for 2 hours, after which the meat should be tender. Taste for seasoning.

If you like, you can make up some *canederli* (dumplings, see page 16), to serve alongside the stew.

2kg piece of **venison leg**
6 tbsp **olive oil**
100g **speck**
50g dried **porcini** (ceps), soaked for 30 minutes then drained and chopped
2 tbsp **tomato paste**, diluted with 2 tbsp **water**
salt and freshly ground **black pepper**

MARINADE
1 litre **red wine**
3 tbsp **cider vinegar**
1 **carrot**
1 **celery stalk**
1 **onion**
3 **bay leaves**
1 little muslin bag holding a couple of **cloves**, 10 **juniper berries** and the rind of 1 **orange**
freshly grated **nutmeg**
a pinch of **powdered cinnamon**

SERVES 6

Game *Carluccio*

In the past, hunting game was a natural way of putting food on the table – and this is still a way of life for many Italian men. Hunting is carefully regulated now, though, as there might soon be nothing left. We now go for bigger game birds: pheasants, partridges, quails, pigeons and wild duck. Furred game includes rabbit, hare, deer, boar and the wild goat that inhabit the high Alpine valleys.

1 **hare**, chopped into medium-sized chunks, including liver, kidneys and ribs
salt and freshly ground **black pepper**
plain flour, for dusting
150ml **extra virgin olive oil**
1 **garlic head**, cloves separated and left whole
a bunch of **rosemary** sprigs
150ml **white wine**

BRUSCHETTA
a few slices of good country **bread**
garlic cloves
extra virgin olive oil, for drizzling

SERVES 4

CONTALDO

Lepre con Aglio e Rosmarino, Servito con Bruschetta
HARE WITH GARLIC AND ROSEMARY, SERVED WITH BRUSCHETTA

Hare is a prize catch for every Italian hunter, whether from the woods, mountains or plains, and is cooked in many different ways all around the country. This simple rustic dish is made in just one large frying pan. You can substitute the meat for rabbit, chicken or guinea fowl if you prefer. Use good extra virgin olive oil for this recipe as quite a lot is used and you really taste its flavour.

Season the hare chunks with salt and pepper and dust with plain flour. In a large, heavy-based frying pan, heat the oil. When hot, add the hare and seal well on all sides until golden-brown and quite crisp. Reduce the heat to low, add the garlic and rosemary, cover with a lid and cook for 45 minutes until tender, turning the meat from time to time. Raise the heat to high, remove the lid, add the wine and allow the liquid to evaporate. Remove from the heat.

To make the bruschetta, toast some slices of country bread, immediately rub with garlic and drizzle with some of the oil. Serve the hare accompanied by the bruschetta.

L'Arte di Arrangiarsi

THE REFLEXIVE VERB *ARRANGIARSI* – LITERALLY MEANING 'TO ARRANGE ONESELF' – COULD NOT BE MORE ITALIAN. The phrase *l'arte di arrangiarsi*, perceived as an 'art', in general represents a philosophy which enjoins Italians to make the most of a difficult situation using all possible means. The 'art of arranging oneself', it describes a talent for being able to reach into oneself and discover hidden resources, something that is very important to Italians. They like to succeed in any endeavour, to have the satisfaction of solving a problem in every possible arena, by using intelligence, cunning, savoir-faire – and this way of thinking applies to all echelons of society, from top to bottom. Like *la bella figura* – which is what 'arranging oneself' eventually leads to (see page 112) – it is a way of life in Italy.

The concept of *arrangiarsi* is almost impossible to translate into other languages as there are a multitude of potential interpretations. In English it could mean: 'to make a virtue of necessity'; 'to grin and bear it'; 'to get by'; 'to create something from nothing'. But these just skim the surface of the many layers of meaning. As with *la bella figura*, centuries of successive foreign conquests and hardship have taught Italians to have no faith in any powers above (apart from God), and that the art of survival is a personal one. To solve the dilemmas and problems of daily life, the Italians have to rely on themselves, on their own inner resourcefulness. I have this problem, how can I solve it? The answer from others might be – and this underlines the attitude – '*Arrangiati*' which means 'I don't know, it is your problem, get on with it.'

When we visited the more inhospitable areas of the Italian Alps, we saw northern Italians are masters at making the best of a difficult situation, a prime example of Italian *arrangiarsi*. Although little can be reliably grown in the high valleys and dishes are fairly basic, because foods are stored, preserved, caught or foraged, they are able to make a nourishing whole. *Pizzoccheri*, for instance, (see page 30) is typical of this: buckwheat pasta, potatoes, cabbage, cheese and butter. It is something born of necessity, and may not be good-looking, but tastes like heaven. (Especially if you drink the local Grumello or Sassella wine with it…) Gennaro's potato and cabbage bake (see page 58) follows the same concept.

These dishes speak of people struggling for survival, who compensate for the lack of ingredients with *arrangiarsi*. Indeed, during the war, foraging was often the only food supply for the *compagni*, or partisans, who hid in the mountains while they fought to liberate Italy from the Nazis. Meanwhile at home, the women became skilled in the more devious aspects of *arrangiarsi*; behaving hospitably towards the unsuspecting enemy (and ignored simply for being women), they would pick up key information about plans, which they would then pass on to their compatriots.

I will now describe a few personal examples of *l'arte di arrangiarsi*. The first that comes to mind is the struggle I endured whilst studying in Vienna, aged twenty (the first time I was away from home). I could not cook, but wanted to recreate the food my mother had produced for me and my five siblings during and after World War Two. Her concoctions, born of necessity and limited by wartime restrictions, were simple, but held such amazing taste memories for me. One such dish was *pasta e patate*, an unlikely marriage of two starches, with flavour provided only by pork lard, a little celery and garlic. These were the only ingredients she could afford to use but these meals were my blueprint, and from them I was able to teach myself to cook, using only my memory and my tastebuds – and occasionally the telephone. This *arrangiarsi* was the beginning of my culinary career.

Another example features my brother and sister-in-law while they were making salami. They mistakenly put sugar instead of salt into the minced meat. Instead of throwing the meat away, they added judicious amounts of salt to the meat, and proceeded with the salami-making. They actually discovered that the resultant salami tasted delicious, one of their best.

I think this is very common – and not just in Italian cooking – that by accident, or through the need to substitute an ingredient, you come up with something different, perhaps even tastier than the original. I've done this myself: if I haven't got all the ingredients I need for a particular dish, I substitute. No fresh tomatoes? I use a can or some tomato paste. No pork for a soup? Put in some bacon or ham instead. Many Italian recipes emanate from the idea of 'making something out of nothing': meatballs made from leftover meat, pasta sauces from leftover vegetables or the juices from a roast chicken. In a sense, *arrangiarsi* lies at the heart of all good Italian cooking.

Gennaro is, I think, the human embodiment of *arrangiarsi*. This is not surprising, considering that we northern Italians consider southerners to be much more skilled at it than we are – the south has always been poorer than the north, and people are obliged to scrape a living out of what they can grow, forage or 'acquire'. The Campanians practically invented the concept, and Naples is ruled by it. In this crowded city, it's dog eat dog, and people 'get by' through practices at best informal, at the very least illicit – tax evasion, unlicenced businesses, smuggling. (And, of course, there are powerful organised crime networks still in operation in the city.)

Gennaro and I first met when he presented himself at the back door of my Neal Street restaurant with a basket of wild mushrooms, gathered from the wooded glades of Walthamstow. He had seen me on television extolling the virtues of the 'quiet hunt'. Thinking I would not consider him worthy if he were revealed to be from the south, he tried to disguise his heavy accent, pretending that he came from the more fashionable Tuscany ('Chianti-shire'). I wasn't deceived however, and yet still I took him on. And thus began our turbulent 30-year relationship…

8 pure **pork sausages**, preferably
   Italian
salt and freshly ground **black
   pepper**
3 tbsp **olive oil**

SAUERKRAUT
1 **Savoy cabbage**, cut into very
   thin strips
1 litre **apple juice**
1 little muslin bag, holding ½ tsp
   whole **black peppercorns**
   and 1 tsp **juniper berries**
1 tbsp **granulated sugar**
50ml **white wine vinegar**

SERVES 4

Carluccio

Crauti con Salsicce
SAUERKRAUT WITH SAUSAGES

*Another recipe from the borders of Italy with Austria, Germany
and Croatia. I don't like how 'Kraut' has become such a derogatory
word, when the cabbage ('kraut' in German) and other relatives of
the Brassica family are given the highest gastronomical praise by
me. Sauerkraut – which will have been salted and fermented – can
of course be bought in jars, but it's so easy to make a fresh version of
your own, which will be full of texture and flavour.*

Put all the sauerkraut ingredients into a large saucepan with a lid.
Bring to the boil, then reduce the heat and cover. Braise, stirring from
time to time, for 20 minutes.

Meanwhile, add the sausages to a pan of lightly salted water and boil,
covered, for 15 minutes. Drain well.

Taste the sauerkraut for seasoning and texture: you want a little bit of
crunch still. If you need more moisture, add some more apple juice.
Remove the muslin bag and season with salt and pepper.

When the sauerkraut is ready, fry the drained sausages in the oil in a
frying pan until brown on all sides. Serve together, accompanied by
some good country bread.

650g **Savoy cabbage**

8 **potatoes**, peeled and thinly sliced

150g **butter**

salt and freshly ground **black pepper**

300g **Taleggio cheese**, thinly sliced

SERVES 4

CONTALDO

Tortino di Patate e Cavolo
POTATO AND CABBAGE BAKE

A lovely combination of potatoes, cabbage and the Alpine cow's cheese, Taleggio. Simple to prepare, and delicious eaten as a side dish with meat, or even on its own.

Preheat the oven to 200°C/Gas 6.

Boil the cabbage and potatoes in separate saucepans in plenty of slightly salted water. Cook the cabbage for about 5 minutes until tender but still crisp. Drain well, rinse in cold water, drain again and squeeze out any excess water with your hands. Pat dry on kitchen paper. Cook the potatoes for 3 minutes, then drain, place in cold water, drain again and dry well on kitchen paper.

Grease an ovenproof dish generously with some of the butter, arrange half of the potato slices, slightly overlapping, on the bottom of the dish, dot with some more butter and season with salt and pepper. Arrange the cabbage leaves, half of the cheese, season, then top with the remaining potatoes and cheese. Dot with the remaining butter. Cover with foil and bake for 25 minutes, removing the foil 5 minutes before the end of the cooking time. Remove from the oven and serve.

Cabbage CONTALDO

Although cabbage is grown all over Italy it has always been a staple of the northern regions, providing nourishment in times of hardship. Despite its somewhat underrated reputation, I have always loved cabbage and it has really evolved in Italian cooking over the years. There are different types: *verza* (Savoy), *cappuccio* (white), *rosso* (red) and *cavolo nero* (black). Savoy cabbage is probably the most used in Italian cooking: in soups, braised with pancetta, or stuffed. White cabbage is used to fill ravioli, in salads and can be braised. Red cabbage is really only known in the north-east of Italy and cooked in local dishes with a Germanic influence. The 'trendy' *cavolo nero*, grown mainly in Tuscany, is similar in taste to Savoy and can be used in much the same way.

250g fresh whole **chestnuts**
4 tbsp **extra virgin olive oil**
1 small **onion**, finely chopped
50g **pancetta**, finely chopped
800g **Savoy cabbage**, chopped
    into thin strips
1 large **apple**, peeled, cored and
    roughly chopped
salt and freshly ground **black
    pepper**
350ml **vegetable stock**

SERVES 4

Verza con Castagne e Mele
CABBAGE WITH CHESTNUTS AND APPLE

Cabbage and chestnuts were often the only foods available when times were hard, and the two would often be combined with stock and eaten as a soup. In fact, my grandparents used to tell us stories of those difficult times and would threaten us with this dish if we were naughty – little did they know that I like cabbage, and that chestnuts are one of my favourite foods! Here I have added some apple as a bit of twist. Serve it simply on its own with lots of bread or as a tasty side dish to accompany meat and game dishes.

With a sharp knife, make an incision in each of the chestnuts. Bring a saucepan of slightly salted water to the boil, add the chestnuts and cook for about 25 minutes. Drain, allow to cool a little, then peel.

In a large saucepan, heat the oil. Sweat the onion, add the pancetta and stir-fry for a few minutes until the pancetta turns golden. Add the cabbage strips, apple, some salt and pepper and the stock. Reduce the heat to medium, cover with a lid and cook for 20 minutes. 5 minutes before the end of the cooking time, stir in the peeled chestnuts. Remove from the heat and serve.

8 very ripe **apricots**, pitted
8 **sugar cubes**
60g **unsalted butter**
2 tbsp dried **breadcrumbs**
½ tbsp **ground cinnamon**
icing sugar, for dusting

DOUGH
60g floury **potatoes**
4 tbsp **caster sugar**
100g **plain flour**
1 **egg yolk**
salt

SERVES 4

Carluccio

Knödeln con Albicocche
APRICOT DUMPLINGS

One of the most delightful dishes I experienced when staying in Vienna was marillenknödel *– apricot dumplings. At the world-famous Sacher Hotel, apricots are stuffed with marzipan-wrapped almonds, then encased in a semolina and cream cheese dough before being boiled. I have simplified the recipe slightly here. The idea of enclosing fruit in a dumpling pastry is known in Switzerland as well, but is particularly popular in northern Italy (that border influence again), where they are sometimes known as* canederli.

To make the dough, cook the potatoes in slightly salted water until soft. Peel and then sieve them or put them through a potato ricer (better than mashing or blending). Add the sugar, flour, egg and a pinch of salt, and mix to a pliable dough.

Meantime bring a large pan of water to the boil, and keep at a simmer. Take a little dough mixture into your hand, enough to cover the palm, and pat it flat. Put an apricot into the centre, and then put a sugar cube into the cavity. Seal the dough around the apricot. Do the same with the remaining dough, apricots and sugar cubes.

Cook the dumplings in batches. Plunge a few at a time into the boiling water and cook for a few minutes until they come to the surface. Scoop out of the water, and keep warm.

In a frying pan, melt the butter and fry the breadcrumbs with the cinnamon. Serve the dumplings hot, sprinkled with the breadcrumbs and some icing sugar.

Carluccio

Mascarpone all' Amaretto
CREAM CHEESE WITH AMARETTO

500g fresh **mascarpone**
4 tbsp **milk**, if required
100g **caster sugar**
50ml **Amaretto** (almond liqueur)
4 **amaretti biscuits**, crumbled
4 **chocolate/amaretti sticks**

SERVES 4

I grew up loving mascarpone, which has its origins in the southern parts of Lombardy. Although called 'cheese', it is rarely used as such: it's really cream coagulated with citric or tartaric acid, and has a silky texture halfway between double cream and butter. When I was a child my mother used to buy just a little at a time because of the cost, treating it with some sugar and egg yolk to give it – and us – a burst of energy. Today I use it in various ways in cooking (in ravioli fillings, in sauces, as the basis of the famous tiramisù), but still love it raw with some added flavourings like this.

Stir the mascarpone in a bowl to soften, adding a little milk if necessary. Add the sugar and Amaretto, and stir to achieve a creamy and smooth texture.

Divide between serving dishes, sprinkle with the crumbled amaretti biscuits and serve with chocolate or amaretti sticks.

4 large **apples**, such as Golden
  Delicious
a pinch of **ground cinnamon**
4 **walnuts**, finely chopped
60g **raisins**
4 **amaretti biscuits**, crushed
4 tbsp runny **honey**
100ml hot **water**

SERVES 4

CONTALDO

Mele al Forno con Noci, Uvetta e Miele
BAKED APPLES WITH WALNUTS, RAISINS AND HONEY

*I love apples and look forward to autumn when they are plentiful.
Italian apples are grown in the fertile valleys of Piedmont, Veneto,
Lombardy and Campania, but the majority come from Trentino-
Alto Adige. The Valle di Non commonly known as 'Valle delle
Mele' (apple valley) produces some fourteen varieties of excellent
quality thanks to its ideal cool climate blessed with lots of sunshine.
Combined with the first walnuts of the season, they make this
simple but delicious dessert.*

Preheat the oven to 200°C/Gas 6. Wash the apples and dry with a cloth.
With a small sharp knife, cut around the top of each apple in a circle.
Remove these tops and set aside. Using a teaspoon or an apple corer,
remove the core from the larger part of the apple.

Divide the cinnamon between each apple. Combine the walnuts,
raisins and crushed biscuits and fill the apples. Spoon a tablespoon of
honey over each apple, and close with the apple top or 'hat'.

Pack the apples tightly together in an ovenproof dish so they don't fall
over. Pour the hot water into the bottom of the dish. Cover with foil
and bake in the preheated oven for 30 minutes until tender, removing
the foil after 15 minutes.

Remove, leave to rest for a couple of minutes and serve with creamy
mascarpone cheese.

200g **unsalted butter**, cut into
  small cubes, plus
  extra for greasing
200g **caster sugar**
300g **quick-cook polenta flour**
100g **plain flour**
finely grated zest of 1 **lemon**
salt
2 **whole eggs**, plus 1 **egg yolk**

MAKES 30–40 BISCUITS

Carluccio

Biscotti di Polenta
POLENTA BISCUITS

Maize, grown in the great northern plain, is ground to flour, which is not only used for making the savoury polenta, but also for cakes and biscuits. I created this biscuit, which is crunchy and so full of flavour that it can be served at any time – as a biscuit for morning coffee or afternoon tea by itself, or as an accompaniment for ice-cream, pannacotta, mascarpone with Amaretto (see page 63) and many more creamy puddings.

Preheat the oven to 190–200°C/Gas 5–6. Grease a large baking tray with a little butter.

In the bowl, mix the butter cubes with the sugar, flours, lemon zest and a pinch of salt and crumble with your fingers until you have a breadcrumb texture. Make a well in the centre. Beat the eggs and egg yolk until well blended, and add to the well in the flour-butter mixture. Mix together to obtain a soft and even consistency.

Spoon the mixture into a piping bag fitted with a 1.5cm nozzle. Squeeze dots of dough on the baking tray, leaving space to allow them to spread. (You may need to bake the biscuits in two batches.) Bake for 15 minutes until golden brown. Allow to cool for a few minutes on the sheet, then using a spatula or fish slice place on a wire rack to cool completely before serving.

250g good-quality **dark chocolate**, broken into small chunks
125g **butter**, plus extra for greasing
4 **egg yolks**
50g **sugar**
6 **egg whites**
salt

SERVES 6

Tortino al Cioccolato Caldo
WARM MINI CHOCOLATE PUDDINGS

When you're in that chocolate mood, this quick and simple dessert, made with some of Turin's finest chocolate, will surely hit the spot. The puddings are best eaten straight away, however you can always heat them up from cold for a few seconds in the microwave or in a hot oven instead if necessary.

Preheat the oven to 180°C/Gas 4. Lightly grease 6 x 6cm ramekin dishes with butter.

Melt the chocolate and butter in a bowl over a pan of gently simmering water.

In a second bowl, whisk the egg yolks with 30g of the sugar until creamy. Stir in the melted chocolate and butter.

In another clean bowl, whisk the egg whites with the remaining sugar and a pinch of salt until stiff. Fold into the chocolate mixture until well amalgamated.

Divide the mixture between the ramekin dishes and bake in the oven for 6 minutes. Remove from the oven, tip the puddings out onto individual plates or leave in the ramekin dishes and serve immediately.

1kg fresh whole **chestnuts**
salt
450g **golden syrup**
1 **vanilla pod**, split in half
350g **caster sugar**

MAKES 3 X 600G JARS

Carluccio

Marmellata di Castagne
CHESTNUT JAM

My granny, Donna Peppinella, was a very good country cook and her chestnut jam, given to us as children after school for merenda *(afternoon snack), still remains in my memory. The jam was seasonal, of course, made in the autumn when the chestnut trees were groaning with fruit. (Sadly, many chestnut trees are dying through disease now, particularly in the north of Italy, though great efforts are being made to save them.) Although the preparation for making this jam is a little elaborate and takes a little patience, your efforts will be well worthwhile.*

Pierce the chestnuts and place in a pan. Cover completely with water and add a pinch of salt. Bring to the boil and cook for 1 hour. Drain them, then leave to cool a little before peeling off the first layer of tough brown shell and as much of the papery brown skin as possible.

Put them back in the pan, cover with water and boil for another 10 minutes. Drain, cool a little, then peel off the remaining pieces of skin. Put the chestnuts into a processor or blender and blend to a fine pulp.

In another pan gently heat the golden syrup, 2 tablespoons of water, the vanilla pod and sugar. When the sugar has melted and you have a syrup, mix in the chestnut pulp. Cook for another 10 minutes.

Spoon into warm sterilised jars, and keep for up to a year (if you can resist eating it within the first couple of weeks!). It can also be used for filling ravioli or tarts.

Nuts Carluccio

With their high content of proteins and healthy oils, nuts are much appreciated in Italy. Most are used in confectionery and sticky cakes, but pistachios and chestnuts are used in soups and pastas. (My mother used to put hot chestnuts in my pockets in winter to keep my hands warm going to school.) Chestnut flour is used in gnocchi, pasta, bread and cakes. When fresh, almonds are minced to make a heavenly drink, *latte di mandorle*; ground, they are the main ingredient of marzipan and frangipane (their shells are used as fuel). Hazelnuts are used similarly. Pine nuts or kernels are used in *pesto genovese*; walnuts in a Ligurian pasta sauce. Walnut and hazelnut oils make wonderful dressings.

FRESH FLAVOURS
from the coast

ITALY IS ALMOST ENTIRELY SURROUNDED BY SEAS – THE MEDITERRANEAN, ADRIATIC, TYRRHENIAN AND IONIAN. The majority of regions have access to the sea except for the landlocked Lombardy, Piedmont, Trentino-Alto Adige and Val d'Aosta in the north, and Umbria in central Italy. The coastlines around Italy cover some 7,600 kilometres, so it is no wonder that the sea has played a crucial role in the country's history.

Carluccio

I will never forget a pasta I ate in Positano, with patelle e cozze *(limpets and mussels). It was so good, I had to have two platefuls…*

The Romans developed trade routes across the Mediterranean and up to the Black Sea, building lighthouses, safe harbours and protecting other seafarers from pirates. The country's proximity to the sea also made it vulnerable to attacks from other countries and, over the centuries, the regions that make up the Italy of today were conquered and ruled by many other nations – one reason for the diversity of its regional cuisines.

The Middle Ages saw the rise of the great Maritime Republics, notably Venice, Genoa, Pisa and Amalfi. Venice and Genoa became Europe's main gateways to trade with the East, and thus were directly responsible for the introduction of many of the eastern flavourings and spices unknown until then – including sugar. And Christopher Columbus, a son of Genoa, in seeking a westerly route to Asia to gain access to the valuable spices of the East, inadvertently discovered islands off America – among them the Bahamas, Hispaniola and Dominica. His refusal to accept that these lands claimed for Spain were not part of Asia might be the reason why America – which in effect he had discovered – was named after the Florentine explorer, Amerigo Vespucci, and not him.

The sea plays a major role in Italian life, and seafood therefore forms a large part of the Italian diet. Geography and climate affect not only the type of seafood caught but also the ingredients used in cooking it. For example, in Veneto in the cooler north, where rice is grown, seafood is commonly served with risotto, while further south it would accompany pasta. In Campania and other southern regions, where it is very much warmer, tomatoes and tomato-based sauces are added to fish dishes like *sarago all'acqua pazza* (sea bream) and *merluzzo alla pizzaiola* (cod) as well as heat-loving vegetables like sweet peppers and aubergines. In Sicily fish is often combined with citrus fruits, which grow there in abundance, having been introduced, centuries ago, by the Arabs.

Every region, even every town has its own variation of a fish soup or stew, known by different names in their own local dialects: *burrida* in Liguria (very similar to the neighbouring Provençal *bouillabaisse* and *bourride*); *cacciucco* in Tuscany; *brodetto* from Venice and the Adriatic. Each uses different fish – *gallinella* (dogfish) in Emilia-Romagna and San Pietro (John Dory) in Marche – and different flavourings (some with tomato, vinegar, saffron or, in the south, sometimes very fiery chilli). Further south, on the Naples coast, you will find *impepata di cozze e vongole* (a type of soup with mussels and clams); on the west coast of Sicily, *ghiotta trapanese*, a broth of seafood served with couscous, another ingredient left by the invading Arabs of centuries ago.

All along Italy's coastline, restaurants specialise in local fish dishes, and it is quite usual to have *antipasto di pesce* (a starter of fish dishes), a pasta or risotto with fish or seafood, and huge platefuls of the popular *fritto misto*, mixed seafood covered in a delicate batter, served with lots of lemon. Geography again plays a role in the fish that are offered: swordfish, anchovies and tuna are plentiful in the south, in Calabria and Sicily. A paste of new-born fish and chilli, *sardella*, is spread on toast in Calabria, or used to dress pasta. On the other side of the Italian boot, because it is shallower and warmer, the Adriatic offers a multitude of shellfish and cephalopods such as *vongole* (clams), crabs, prawns, cuttlefish and squid (some of them, seen in the Rialto market in Venice, sold heartbreakingly small).

Fish was traditionally preserved by salting, marinating, air-drying and, more recently, canning. Today this has become a lucrative business, valuable not only to those who live far from the sea and have no access to fresh fish but also because these fish have become key ingredients in daily cooking throughout Italy. Preserved anchovies, for instance, form the base of many dishes; preserved tuna is added to pasta and salads. Although not from Italian coasts, *baccalà* and *stoccafisso*, respectively salted and air-dried cod, have to be mentioned, as they are widely used. Preserved cod was first introduced to Italy during the Middle Ages, possibly by the Normans, who were of course from Scandinavia. At first it was a food of the poor, useful because it could be eaten on fast days (when no meat was allowed), but over time salt cod has become highly prized (and expensive) and is now eaten only on special occasions. In Venice, *baccalà mantecato* is a speciality, as is *baccalà con pomodoro e patate* in the Naples area; *stoccafisso alla genovese*, made with locally-grown Taggiasca olives, comes from Genoa, and a Tuscan speciality is *baccalà livornese*.

CONTALDO
Once, on the Sicilian island of Lipari, I preserved freshly caught anchovies to bring home to England. My family still preserve anchovies and tuna in the traditional way at home in the south.

Carluccio

Mandilli di Seta
SILK HANDKERCHIEF PASTA WITH PESTO

This particular dish is very characteristic of one of the most interesting coastal regions of Italy – Liguria. It must be something to do with the air, but the best basil in Italy grows here, usually the small-leaved type, thus the famous sauce, pesto al Genovese (from Genoa). Both pasta and pesto are best made at home from scratch – only in this way will you obtain the desired taste and texture.

To make the pasta, place the flour in a bowl or on a work surface, and make a well in the centre. Add the egg, yolks, half the oil and a pinch of salt. Firstly with a fork and then with your hands, gradually mix the flour with the eggs and oil until you obtain a rough paste. If necessary, add a splash of water. Knead the dough on a lightly floured surface for a few minutes until it is smooth, not sticky. Cover with a cloth and leave to rest for 15–30 minutes.

Divide the dough into quarters. If you have a pasta machine, put the dough through the rollers gradually, starting with the highest setting, until you have silky sheets about 1mm thick, or less. Cut the sheets of pasta into large squares, about 15 x 15cm, and dust with flour to prevent them sticking together.

To make the pesto, put the basil leaves in a large mortar with the salt, pine kernels and garlic. Grind down with the pestle until it becomes a fine pulp. Start to add the oil and continue grinding until the mixture is smooth. Add the Parmesan and mix well.

Put the pasta sheets one by one into a saucepan with plenty of lightly salted boiling water and add the remaining oil. Cook until *al dente*, about 3 minutes or so.

Put about 3–4 tablespoons of pesto in a large pan and warm up gently with the same amount of water from the pasta pan, which will dilute it a bit. Remove the pasta sheets from the water using a perforated scoop and put them into the sauce. Add the rest of the sauce, mix well, and serve with a few extra basil leaves to garnish.

250g Italian **'00' flour**, plus extra for dusting
1 **egg**, plus 3 **egg yolks**
2 tbsp **olive oil**
salt

PESTO
a large bunch of small-leaved **basil**, about 50 leaves
10–15g coarse **sea salt**
40g **pine kernels**
4 **garlic cloves**, peeled
100ml **olive oil**
80g **Parmesan** or pecorino, freshly grated

SERVES 4

300g *fregola*
salt and freshly ground **black pepper**
4 tbsp **olive oil**
2 **garlic cloves**, very finely sliced
200g **red mullet fillets**, cut into pieces
125ml dry **white wine**
400g crushed **fresh tomatoes** or tinned
a small pinch of **cayenne pepper**
1kg **black mussels**
2 tbsp chopped **flat-leaf parsley**

SERVES 4

Carluccio

Fregola con Cozze
SARDINIAN PASTA WITH MUSSELS

Fregola *is a type of durum wheat pasta which is found only in Sardinia. (There is a local saying that a girl is only marriageable if she can produce perfect* fregola!*) You can buy packets of* fregola, *little pellets of dry pasta, in good Italian delicatessens but in Sardinia it is also available fresh – made by hand – looking like giant grains of couscous. Its origins could be African and it is thought to have been introduced by the Ancient Romans. Served with mussels it is very delicious.*

Cook the fregola in plenty of lightly salted boiling water for 10 minutes or until *al dente*. Drain and set aside.

Heat the oil in a large saucepan and fry the garlic until cooked but not brown. Add the fish pieces and fry for a couple of minutes then add the wine and tomatoes. Season with salt, pepper and a touch of cayenne and cook for 5–6 minutes.

Clean the mussels thoroughly, scrubbing them in cold water and removing the beards. Add the cleaned mussels to the fish, put the lid on the pan and cook for a few minutes until the mussels open.

Add the *fregola* and parsley to the pan and mix well. Divide between deep plates and eat with spoons and fingers.

1kg **clams**
salt and freshly ground **black pepper**
150ml **white wine**
1 **garlic clove**
4 tbsp **extra virgin olive oil**, plus extra for drizzling
a handful of **parsley**, roughly chopped
1g sachet of **powdered saffron**
320g *tubetti* **pasta**
a handful of **rocket**

SERVES 4

Tubetti con Vongole e Rucola
TUBETTI PASTA WITH CLAMS AND ROCKET

Pasta with vongole, or clams, is a classic dish served in most coastal regions throughout Italy. I urge you to make this with fresh clams, which are obtainable from good fishmongers and the fish counters at larger supermarkets. The addition of saffron gives a nice yellow colour to the sauce and the rocket adds extra freshness. Usually spaghetti is served with a clam sauce, but for a change I have used tubetti – small tubes of pasta – which are also good with mussels.

Rinse the clams under cold running water. Place in a bowl with salted cold water and leave for about an hour. You will notice the shells opening slightly. Rinse under cold running water again.

Place the rinsed clams in a large saucepan together with the wine, garlic, oil and parsley. Cover with a lid and cook on a high heat for 3 minutes, until all the shells have opened. Remove from the heat. Immediately discard any unopened clams. Remove two thirds of the clams from their shells, leaving the rest intact. Set aside. Strain the sauce for any impurities, return to the pan with the shelled clams and cook on a medium heat until it reduces slightly. Stir in the saffron.

Meanwhile, bring a saucepan of slightly salted water to the boil, add the pasta and cook until *al dente*. Drain and add to the sauce. Mix in the rocket and season with salt and pepper. Remove from the heat and stir in the clams in the shell. Drizzle with oil and serve immediately.

Spaghetti alla Pizzaiola
SPAGHETTI WITH PIZZAIOLA SAUCE

This sauce originates from Naples and its ingredients are similar to those of a pizza topping, hence its name. Apart from pasta, the sauce is often used to liven up steak and fish. This is a quick and simple pasta dish using the typical store-cupboard ingredients of most Italian households – an ideal meal for unexpected guests.

Heat the oil in a large frying pan. Add the garlic, chilli and anchovy fillets and gently fry until the garlic has softened (not burnt) and the anchovies have dissolved in the oil. Add the olives and capers and cook, stirring, for a minute. Add the tomatoes, oregano, parsley and season with salt to taste. Lower the heat, cover with a lid and simmer gently for 20 minutes.

In the meantime, cook the spaghetti in slightly salted boiling water until *al dente*. Drain, reserving a few tablespoons of the cooking water, and add to the sauce. Stir well and continue to cook for a further minute, so that the pasta absorbs all the flavours. If you find it is too dry, add the hot pasta water. Remove from the heat and serve immediately.

4 tbsp **extra virgin olive oil**
1 **garlic clove**, finely chopped
½ small **red chilli**, finely chopped (optional)
4 **anchovy fillets**
12 **black olives**, sliced in half and pitted or left whole
1 tbsp **capers**
400g tin chopped **tomatoes**
½ tsp dried **oregano**
1 tbsp finely chopped **parsley**
salt
350g **spaghetti**

SERVES 4

200g pre-cooked medium-ground **semolina couscous**
250ml hot **water**
salt and freshly ground **black pepper**
8 tbsp **olive oil**
1 **garlic clove**, sliced
350g *moscardini* (fresh baby octopus), halved if large
125ml dry **white wine**
1 tbsp **tomato paste**, diluted in 125ml water
½ tsp **chilli powder**, or chopped fresh **chilli**
1g sachet of powdered **saffron**
2 tbsp finely chopped **flat-leaf parsley**

SERVES 4

Carluccio

Cuscusu Trapanese
SEAFOOD COUSCOUS

From the town of Trapani in Sicily – an island which has seen many invaders, and many culinary influences – comes this recipe which is unique to the area. Couscous (small pellets of durum wheat semolina) is normally associated with Arab and North African cuisines, where it is usually an accompaniment to meat stews, particularly of lamb. Here it is served with baby octopus, and very delightful it is too.

Put the couscous in a bowl. Pour in the water and a bit of salt, stirring, so that the water is absorbed evenly by the grains. After about 10 minutes, when the grains have plumped up, add 2 tablespoons of the oil and work it in with your fingers. Put the couscous in a couscoussière or the top half of a steamer lined with a cloth. Cover with a lid and cook until the steam is rising through the grains which means the couscous is ready, about 20 minutes.

Meanwhile, heat the remaining oil in a large frying pan, add the garlic and fry until softened. Add the octopus and wine, along with the diluted tomato paste, chilli and saffron, and cook until the octopus is tender, about 10–12 minutes. Season with salt and pepper.

Mix the cooked couscous with the octopus stew, sprinkle with parsley and serve hot.

1.5 litres **vegetable stock**
4 tbsp **extra virgin olive oil**
1 small **onion**, finely chopped
350g **arborio risotto rice**
50ml **white wine**
200g small peeled **prawns**
1 small **courgette**, finely chopped
10 **courgette flowers**, roughly
   torn
a handful of **basil** leaves, roughly
   torn

SERVES 4

CONTALDO

Risotto con Gamberetti e Fiori di Zucchini
RISOTTO WITH PRAWNS AND COURGETTE FLOWERS

Around the coastlines of Italy it is not uncommon to enjoy risotto with seafood, especially in the Venetian lagoon. Here the delicate courgette flowers combine beautifully with the sweetness of the prawns and the fresh basil leaves. In southern Italy we consume a lot of courgettes and their flowers during the spring, when this vegetable is at its very best.

Bring the stock to the boil in a saucepan and keep it at a low simmer.

In a separate saucepan, heat half the oil, add the onion and sweat until softened. Stir in the rice, coating each grain with the oil. Add the wine and keep stirring until it evaporates. Stir in the prawns and courgette. Then start to add the stock, ladle by ladle, waiting until each ladleful has been absorbed before you add next. Continue to do this for about 15–20 minutes until the rice is cooked *al dente*. About 5 minutes before the end of the cooking time, stir in the courgette flowers.

Remove from the heat and beat in the remaining oil and the basil. Serve immediately.

Islands

WHEN WE THINK OF THE ITALIAN ISLANDS, SICILY AND SARDINIA IMMEDIATELY SPRING TO MIND, but there are many, many more, all of which contribute to the rich diversity of Italian food and culture. Most of Italy's islands share a similar terrain to the mainland, with mountain ranges, plains, forests and jagged coastlines, but fewer rivers and lakes, and most tend to have a drier climate.

Sicily, the largest Italian island is surrounded by the warm waters of the southern Mediterranean and enjoys a very balmy climate all year round. This makes it excellent for growing olives, vines, almonds and citrus fruits – their blood-red oranges are the best in the world! – so it is no wonder Sicilians eat an abundance of fresh vegetables and fruit. Some of the largest tuna and swordfish in Italy are caught along the Sicilian coast, as well as an array of other Mediterranean fish and shellfish.

The islands of Italy have had their fair share of invaders over history. Although only three kilometres from the Italian mainland, Sicily appears far removed in feel and culture. Its strategic position in the Mediterranean made it an easy stopping place for all who sailed the sea: the Greeks, Romans, Arabs, Normans and Spanish all left their mark on Sicilian architecture and culture, but the greatest evidence of their historic presence is in the island's food. Sicilian cuisine is probably the most eclectic in all of Italy. Couscous from North Africa, sauces of *agrodolce* (sweet and sour), and the use of pine kernels, almonds, raisins, cinnamon and other spices – these are mostly Arab-introduced flavours which are very alien to the rest of Italy. These invaders are also responsible for contributing to Sicily's sweet tooth, introducing ice-cream and granita, marzipan and candied fruit, and the delicious ricotta-based dessert, *cassata*.

Despite being surrounded by water, fish has strangely never played a big role in the cuisine of Sardinia. Historically, from fear of invaders, Sardinians preferred to live inland among the remote rugged mountains, tending their sheep (as evidenced in the famous 1977 film *Padre Padrone*). Far removed from mainland Italy, these farmers and shepherds became dependent on what the land provided. Their cooking is regarded as *cucina povera* (poor man's cuisine), but the ingredients have always been of an excellent quality. A pasta, *malloreddus*, is a shape unique to the island as

are *culurzones*, a type of ravioli filled with pecorino and potato, and *fregola*, large semolina granules similar to couscous and eaten as pasta. Meat features heavily in the Sardinian diet, particularly inland, and excellent lamb, mutton, goat and pork dishes like *porceddu* (roast suckling pig) can be enjoyed. The hillsides are full of herbs and bushes like *mirto*, myrtle, which is not only used to flavour cooking but is made into a famous Sardinian liqueur. There is also an amazing array of cheese made from sheep and goat's milk – including the famous *pecorino sardo* – and many local breads, one of which is *pane carasau*, a wafer-thin flatbread traditionally made for shepherds to take with them in the mountains as, dried, it lasted for longer.

Nowadays Sardinians do of course enjoy the coast and eat all the usual array of Mediterranean fish and shellfish. But it is Sardinia's *bottarga*, preserved tuna roe, which is renowned and highly prized, especially when delicately shaved over pasta dishes. And *mosciame*, air-dried tuna, is served as a light *antipasto*, or pre-meal snack, on the menus of expensive restaurants.

The third largest Italian island is Elba, just off the Tuscan coast. Mainly occupied on the coast by tourists in the summer months, the interior mountainous areas are home to wild boar. Here fish and shellfish are primarily eaten, and *cacciucco*, the Tuscan fish soup, is as popular now as it was when Napoleon lived here in exile. More unusual foods from the days of invaders are still eaten in certain villages like *schiacca briaca*, a Middle-Eastern sweet bread made with dried fruit and nuts, *imbollita*, a fig focaccia, and *sportella*, aniseed Easter bread.

Travelling south to the Campania region, we come to the famous Partenopean islands of Capri and Ischia. Again, now largely occupied by hordes of tourists, they are like a continuation of the Neapolitan and Amalfi coasts with mountains and lush green coastal plains. Here the food is much influenced by Campania, and the fertile terraces are excellent for growing lemons and vines, the latter producing some great wine, albeit in small quantity. Ischian food tends to be more peasant-like in nature, with dishes like the rabbit stew *coniglio all' Ischitana*: the rabbits for which are traditionally bred in holes in the ground, 'farmed' but as if they were in the wild.

Capri, on the other hand, tends to offer more sophisticated dishes of lobster and langoustine to satisfy the palates of its rich and famous residents and visitors. Not forgetting the renowned *insalata caprese*, a salad using buffalo mozzarella and the sorrentine tomatoes grown on the island. Ischia, with its

thermal springs, is a known retreat for spa holidays, and Capri with its glitz is the ultimate place to show off *la bella figura* (see page 112).

On the other side of Italy's boot, on the Puglian coast, is the archipelago of the Isole Tremiti. These jewels of the Adriatic, part of the Gargano National Park, are wild expanses of dense, luxuriant pine forests with an undergrowth of hardy herbs like juniper, rosemary and myrtle. Not all the islands are inhabited and those that are tend to be mainly for holiday purposes.

And we must not forget the islands of the Venetian laguna, known as *isolotti*, mainly Burano, Murano, Torcello and Giudecca, who rely on the fish of the laguna to eat and sell, not to mention the smaller islands in the lakes, such as the Isole Borromee – Bella, Madre and dei Pescatori – in Lago Maggiore... Yet in spite of the bewildering variety and specialities, the one thing that unites all island cooking is the fact that your ingredients will have been produced within a few miles. Whether it's fish from the coast, cheese and meat from the interior, and a variety of fruit and vegetables, you know that what you eat will be the freshest and taste the best!

CONTALDO

2kg mixed **fresh fish fillets and shellfish,** such as red mullet, small sole, gurnard, monkfish, sea bass, cuttlefish, baby octopus, prawns, mussels, squid or scallops

8 tbsp **olive oil**, plus extra for drizzling

1 large **onion**, finely sliced

2 **garlic cloves**, finely chopped, plus an extra clove for rubbing

1kg ripe **tomatoes**, skinned and chopped, or 2 x 400g tins of chopped tomatoes

125ml **red wine**

a little chopped fresh **chilli**

3 tbsp finely chopped **flat-leaf parsley**

½ tsp **fennel seeds**

salt and freshly ground **black pepper**

6–8 slices good **bread**, slightly stale or toasted

SERVES 6–8

Carluccio

Cacciucco
FISH SOUP-STEW

The Italian equivalent of the French bouillabaisse has an infinity of variations and is known by different names depending on the region, town or village in Italy you visit. Traditionally, no fewer than five types of fish go into this cacciucco *from the port of Livorno in Tuscany. One for every 'C' in the name...*

If your fishmonger hasn't already done so, clean and prepare your chosen fish and shellfish. Cut fish fillets into large chunks and seafood into manageable pieces.

Put the oil, onion and garlic into a large pan and fry briefly. Add the tomatoes, wine, chilli, parsley and fennel seeds and season with salt and pepper. Cook for 15 minutes. Start to add large pieces of fish to the sauce first and those that will take the longest to cook, such as monkfish, then add the more tender fish such as red mullet or sole and the shellfish, ending up with the mussels if using. Cook for 5 or so minutes, or until the fish is cooked and the mussels have opened.

Rub the bread with garlic, drizzle with olive oil, and put each slice in the bottom of a deep soup bowl. Pour over the soup. *Buon appetito.*

8 small whole **red mullet**, about
   150g each, gutted and scaled
plain flour, for coating
salt and freshly ground **black
   pepper**
6 tbsp **olive oil**
1 small **onion**, finely sliced
1 **garlic clove**, finely sliced
2 tbsp chopped **flat-leaf parsley**
3 **anchovy fillets**
30g dried **porcini** (ceps), soaked
   for 30 minutes then drained
   and chopped
300g tin of chopped **tomatoes**

SERVES 4

Carluccio

Triglie alla Genovese
RED MULLET WITH TOMATO, ANCHOVY AND PORCINI SAUCE

*When you see on a menu 'alla Genovese' or 'alla Bolognese', it
means that the dish is typically cooked in the nominated area, place
or town (in the above examples, Genoa and Bologna). This red
mullet dish is very popular in Genoa, the vast sea port of Liguria,
using the locally caught fish, which are very tasty. It is best made
with small mullet, which may be more bony, but are much tastier.*

Dust the fish inside and out with flour and season with salt and
pepper. Shake off any excess flour. Heat the oil in a large frying pan
and fry the fish until golden on each side, about 3–4 minutes. Set to
one side.

In the same pan, fry the onion, garlic, parsley, anchovies and soaked
porcini for 5 minutes, then add the tomatoes and season with salt and
pepper to taste. Cook for a further 10 minutes.

Return the fish to the pan and heat through in the sauce for a few
minutes to finish. Serve with some good bread or a purée of potatoes.

CONTALDO

Cefalo al Mediterraneo
GREY MULLET WITH CHERRY TOMATOES AND BASIL

Grey mullet is a prized fish in Italy found on every coastline, but particularly in river estuaries. This is a popular way of cooking fish in southern Italy: the ingredients are typically Mediterranean, encompassing the taste of the sea and the flavours of the sunny south. The trick of this dish is to have very fresh ingredients and good-quality extra virgin olive oil – the rest is simple.

Heat the oil in a large heavy-based frying pan over a high heat. Add the grey mullet followed by the garlic, tomatoes, olives, basil, chilli and a little salt. Pour in the water, reduce the heat to medium and cook for about 8 minutes on each side. (If the fish eye has turned white, you will know it is done and that it is time to flip over to the other side.)

Remove the fish from the pan and place on a large serving dish. Increase the heat and cook the sauce for about 30 seconds to reduce slightly, then pour over the fish. Serve immediately with lots of bread to mop up the delicious sauce.

170ml **extra virgin olive oil**
2 whole **grey mullet**, about 500g each, gutted and scaled
4 **garlic cloves**, finely sliced
200g **cherry tomatoes**
10 **black olives**
a handful of **basil** leaves, roughly torn
1 small **red chilli**, finely chopped
salt
400ml **water**

SERVES 4

1kg **stocco** (air-dried cod)
500g waxy **potatoes**, peeled and
   sliced
6 tbsp **olive oil**
2 **garlic cloves**, crushed
30g dried **porcini** (ceps), soaked
   for 20 minutes,
   drained and chopped
100g pitted **black olives**
2 tbsp chopped **flat-leaf parsley**

SERVES 6

Carluccio

Stocco con Porcini
DRIED COD AND MUSHROOM STEW

I still find it curious, the Italian love of preserved, air-dried or salted cod, when plenty of fresh, delicious fish is available along every coastline in the country. One reason could be the legacy of explorers like Columbus and others, who were obliged to take on board foods which would last a long time. And, of course, in many landlocked parts of Italy preserved fish has to be eaten, as fresh fish is rarely available. Whatever the reason, this fish has a spectacular taste, and that's what Italians like.

Cut the cod into chunks and place, skin-side up, in a large bowl with plenty of cold water. Soak for at least 24 hours, changing the water every 7–8 hours.

After soaking the fish, drain it and put it in a pan. Cover with fresh cold water, bring to the boil and cook until flaky and the flesh comes off the bone, about 1 hour. Boil the potatoes in the same water for the last 15 minutes.

Heat the olive oil in a large frying pan, and fry the garlic briefly, then add the mushrooms and olives and fry gently for 10 minutes. Add some water if the mixture is looking too dry. Set aside.

Prepare the cod by removing all the skin and bones with your fingers and reducing the flesh to flakes. Mix with the potatoes, parsley and mushroom mix and serve.

4 whole **sea bass**, about 200g
  each, gutted and cleaned
a handful of **flat-leaf parsley**,
  finely chopped
8 **bay leaves**
2 **garlic cloves**, thinly sliced
salt and freshly ground **black
  pepper**
1 **orange**, peel and pith removed,
  sliced
1 **lemon**, peel and pith removed,
  sliced
extra virgin olive oil, for
  drizzling
juice of 1 large **orange**
juice of 1 **lemon**
60ml **white wine**

SERVES 4

CONTALDO

Branzino agli Agrumi
SEA BASS WITH CITRUS FRUIT

Sea bass is a popular fish in Italy, and is caught along most of the coastal areas. This delicate-tasting fish is prepared in many ways – boiled, baked, grilled, even raw – and is always a delight to eat. This dish is simple to prepare and combines the subtle flavours of sun-drenched orange and lemon with the freshness of the sea.

Preheat the oven to 180°C/Gas 4.

Wash the sea bass under a cold running tap and dry with a kitchen cloth. In the slit of each belly, place some parsley, a bay leaf, garlic, salt, pepper and the orange and lemon slices (reserving a few for garnish).

Drizzle a large ovenproof dish with oil and carefully place the fish on top. Pour over the orange and lemon juices and white wine, then scatter with the remaining bay leaves and sprinkle with salt and pepper. Cover with foil and place in the preheated oven for about 25 minutes, until the fish is cooked through. Take off the foil, turn off the heat and leave in the oven for a couple of minutes to rest before removing.

To serve, either fillet each sea bass and divide among individual plates or serve whole. Pour over the juices left in the pan and garnish with the remaining orange and lemon slices.

8 thin slices of **swordfish**, about 100g each
4 tbsp finely chopped **flat-leaf parsley**
2 **garlic cloves**, very finely chopped
50g **Parmesan**, freshly grated
4 tbsp **dried breadcrumbs**
juice of 1 **orange**
salt and freshly ground **black pepper**
plain flour, for coating
4 tbsp **olive oil**
125ml dry **white wine**
1 **lemon**, cut into wedges

SERVES 4

Carluccio

Involtini di Pesce Spada
SWORDFISH ROLLS

In the breeding season the swordfish is a common visitor to the shores of Calabria and Sicily. Swordfish flesh is very sought after because it doesn't taste fishy, and the texture is reminiscent of meat. When buying swordfish for this dish, which is typical of Calabria, be sure to ask your fishmonger to cut the slices thinly so that you can stuff and roll them easily.

Lay the swordfish slices on a work surface. In a bowl, mix the parsley, garlic, Parmesan, breadcrumbs and orange juice. Divide the mix evenly between the fish slices, season with salt and pepper, and roll up. Keep the rolls closed with wooden cocktail sticks and dust them with flour.

Heat the oil in a frying pan and fry the rolls until golden on each side, about 2–3 minutes. Add the wine and heat through. Serve immediately with the lemon wedges.

8 tbsp **extra virgin olive oil**

2 large sweet **red onions,** finely sliced

3 tbsp **red wine vinegar**

400g fresh **tuna**, cut into small chunks

salt

80g **rocket leaves**

200g **baby spinach leaves**

SERVES 4

Insalata di Tonno con Cipolle di Tropea

WARM TUNA SALAD WITH SWEET RED ONIONS

On the southern coast of Italy, especially in Sicily, tuna used to be caught in large quantities. Italians love tuna either canned or fresh, and in the south certain families still preserve their own at home. I enjoy both, and this recipe, using the freshest of tuna, makes a lovely nutritious light meal, enhanced by the sweet onions from Tropea in Calabria. Tuna, however, has been overfished in many waters around Italy, and in many parts, Liguria, for instance, none are now allowed to be landed. When buying it fresh, try to steer clear of Atlantic bluefin tuna in favour of more sustainable varieties such as skipjack or yellowfin.

Heat 6 tablespoons of the oil in a frying pan, add the onions, cover with a lid and sweat gently on a low heat for about 10 minutes until soft. Add the vinegar, tuna and a pinch of salt, and continue to cook on a low heat for about 5 minutes until the tuna is tender.

Meanwhile put the rocket and spinach leaves in a large bowl and sprinkle with salt. Drizzle over the remaining oil and toss to combine. Add the cooked tuna and onions and mix well. Serve immediately.

Onions and Garlic
CONTALDO

I could not imagine cooking without these two key ingredients! They form the basis of most Italian sauces, the *soffritto*. You can have garlic as potent as you like or just a hint in your cooking. Its aroma is released as you cut the cloves, so if you want a pungent dish, you chop finely; for something milder, leave whole, sauté, then discard the clove. Whole cloves can be roasted, giving a mild, sweet taste. I love raw garlic in salad dressings, or with steamed fish, as well as for rubbing on toasted bread to make bruschetta.

4 **garlic cloves**, very finely
  chopped
5 tbsp chopped **flat-leaf parsley**
8 tbsp **olive oil**
6 large **potatoes**, about 800g
  (preferably Desirée),
  peeled and cut into 6–7mm
  slices
salt and freshly ground **black
  pepper**
80g **pecorino cheese**, freshly
  grated
6 **sea bream fillets**, about
  200g each

SERVES 6

Carluccio

Orata alla Pugliese
BAKED FISH WITH POTATOES

*The combination of fish and potatoes has always been attractive,
the potatoes absorbing all the flavours of the fish and herbs.
Orata, or sea bream, is the fish used traditionally in this dish, but
you could use sea bass instead. Fish cooked in this way is typically
Puglian, though when I was once in Venice Conte Maria Rocca
prepared a similar dish for me, using monkfish.*

Preheat the oven to 200°C/Gas 6.

Mix the garlic, parsley and olive oil in a bowl, then pour half of this
into the base of a deep baking tray large enough to hold the fish. Cover
with a layer of half the potato slices, and season with salt and pepper.
Sprinkle with half of the cheese. Put the fish fillets on top, and cover
with the remaining cheese and potato slices. Spread the remaining
parsley and garlic oil on top.

Bake in the preheated oven for 35 minutes until the fish is cooked and
the potato slices are tender. Serve hot.

12 large, plump **oysters**,
  opened, top discarded, and
  the flesh loosened
1 large **garlic clove**, crushed
4 tbsp finely chopped **chives**
4 tbsp finely chopped **parsley**
½ tsp **fennel seeds**
4 **anchovy fillets**, finely chopped
2 tbsp dried **breadcrumbs**
juice of ½ **lemon**
extra virgin olive oil

SERVES 4

Carluccio

Ostriche alla Livornese

BRAISED OYSTERS WITH A HERB, ANCHOVY
AND FENNEL SEED TOPPING

*This is a very curious way to eat oysters – cooked instead of raw.
Although it sounds modern, this recipe goes back some 200 years
and is from Livorno in Tuscany: a very old town which has many
restaurants, snack bars and beach shacks serving fresh fish and
shellfish from the Tyrrhenian Sea. Although I prefer to eat oysters
the usual way, I have learned to appreciate them cooked like this.*

Preheat the grill. Put the oysters on a baking tray that will fit under
the grill. Set aside.

Mix all the remaining ingredients together, apart from the oil. Now
slowly add the oil, stirring, to make a paste consistency. Top each
oyster with a little of the paste and grill for 5–7 minutes. Serve.

Spices *Carluccio*

Herbs are more characteristic of Italian
cooking, but we do use a few spices. Sea
salt is still made in Sicily and Sardinia
and is used for seasoning and making
salami and preserves. Pepper gives a
kick to almost anything, including
strawberries; white pepper, surprisingly,
is more common than black. Capers
are the flower bud of a wild plant and
are salted to counteract bitterness, then
stored in vinegar, brine or salt (my
favourite). Small hot chillies are used
in salami and pasta sauces (famously
in *arrabbiata*, 'angry sauce'). We also
enjoy the pungency of fennel seeds and
occasionally coriander seeds in salami,
biscuits and cakes.

8 tbsp **extra virgin olive oil**
6 **anchovy fillets**
10g **capers**
2 **garlic cloves**, finely sliced
1 small **red chilli**, finely chopped
1kg **squid**, cleaned and chopped
   into quarters
salt
50ml **white wine**
250g **cherry tomatoes**, halved
a handful of **flat-leaf parsley**,
   roughly chopped

SERVES 4

CONTALDO

Calamari in Umido
BRAISED SQUID IN TOMATO

Calamari *or squid, along with its friends the cuttlefish and octopus, are much loved in Italy, and are cooked in a variety of ways depending on region and taste. Some* calamari *can be enormous, weighing several kilos each, though you can also find much smaller* calamaretti *(baby squid). I like to braise squid in tomato sauce like this, though they are equally delicious cooked with potatoes, stuffed and stewed, simply grilled with lemon, or fried as part of a* fritto misto. *In Venice the squid ink is used to colour risotto and pasta – a good example of how Italian cooking wastes nothing.*

Heat the oil in a saucepan, add the anchovies and capers, and cook over a medium heat, stirring, until the anchovies dissolve. Add the garlic and chilli, stir and continue to cook for a couple of minutes.

Add the squid, a pinch of salt and stir-fry for a further couple of minutes. Add the wine and boil until it evaporates. Add the cherry tomatoes and parsley, reduce the heat to low and cook, covered for 45 minutes. Remove from the heat and serve with lots of good bread to mop up the sauce. Delicious.

12 large **mussels**
¼ glass **white wine**
a handful of **dried breadcrumbs**
a handful of **parsley**, finely
  chopped
extra virgin olive oil, plus extra
  for drizzling

FILLING
4 tbsp **extra virgin olive oil**
4 **anchovy fillets**
1 **garlic clove**, finely chopped
½ small **red chilli**, finely chopped
1 tbsp **capers**
a handful of **parsley**, finely
  chopped
100g stale **bread**, cubed
freshly ground **black pepper**

SERVES 4–6

CONTALDO

Cozze Ripiene
FILLED MUSSELS

*Mussels are plentiful all along the coastlines of Italy, and are
farmed in the Venetian lagoon, so it is no wonder they are used
abundantly in many dishes. This southern Italian way of preparing
mussels is often seen in restaurants as part of an antipasto plate
together with other mouthwatering fish and shellfish dishes. I like to
serve them with some salad leaves for a light lunch.*

Preheat the oven to 200°C/Gas 6. Clean the mussels by washing them
under cold running water, scrubbing them well and pulling off the
beards. Place in a saucepan with the wine, cover with a lid and cook on
a high heat for a minute or so until the mussels have opened. Remove
from the heat, strain the liquid and set aside. Remove the mussel flesh
from the opened shells and set aside. Discard any that haven't opened.
Carefully split the opened shells into halves.

To make the filling, heat the oil in a pan, add the anchovies and cook,
stirring, until they have almost dissolved. Lower the heat, add the
garlic, chilli and capers and sweat for a couple of minutes. Stir in the
mussels and heat through. Add 3 tablespoons of the reserved mussel
liquid and half the parsley. Gently simmer for a minute. Remove from
the heat, stir in the bread cubes and pepper and leave to cool.

Place the cooled mixture on a chopping board and finely chop. Place
it in a bowl and stir together well. Fill the shell halves with the mixture
and place on a baking tray. Combine the breadcrumbs with the parsley
and enough oil to moisten slightly. Sprinkle this topping over the
filled mussels and bake in the oven for 15 minutes until golden brown.
Remove, drizzle with some oil and serve.

175ml **extra virgin olive oil**

12 fresh raw **king prawns**, shells on

6 **garlic cloves**, sliced lengthways

1 large **red chilli**, finely chopped

fresh **crab meat** from 2 large crabs, in chunks

salt

a handful of **flat-leaf parsley**

250ml **white wine**

1 **lemon**, cut into wedges

SERVES 4

Gamberoni e Granchio con Aglio e Peperoncino
KING PRAWNS AND CRAB WITH GARLIC AND CHILLI

I remember fishing for crabs in Italy as a child, but they were small, cleaning them was a chore and you had to catch quite a few to make a meal out of them! They were however delicious, and we would often combine them with other seafood and sometimes with pasta. Here the sweetness of the crab and prawn combine excellently with the stronger flavours of garlic and chilli, but make sure you use good oil and the freshest of crab meat. If you prefer, you can omit the crab and replace it with extra prawns.

Heat the oil in a large frying pan, add the king prawns and cook for 2 minutes, turning once. Add the garlic, chilli and crab meat, season with salt, then reduce the heat and cook for a couple of minutes with the lid on. Add the parsley, increase the heat and add the wine and reserved juices from the crab meat if you have any. Bubble until evaporated, then serve immediately with lemon wedges and lots of good country bread to mop up the juices.

La Bella Figura

EVEN BEFORE THE ARTISTS OF THE ITALIAN RENAISSANCE PAINTED GOD IN THEIR OWN IMAGE, and Leonardo da Vinci delineated the figure of a man in a perfect circle, the concept of *la bella figura* – literally 'the beautiful figure' – had begun to resonate in all aspects of Italian life. As early as the 14th century, *la bella figura* formed the basis of codes of honour, thought to be have been introduced by the Romans to the countries they colonised: the honour of the family, group or state was paramount, and bad behaviour dishonoured all. Since then the concept has grown to encompass much more, and in Italy it has become an all-pervading philosophy.

In essence, *la bella figura* is the art of making a good impression, whether privately or in public: for the rich, this can sometimes even be seen as the desire to be publicly envied; for the poor, it is about maintaining dignity in the face of poverty. Although *la bella figura* may start with the physical, it has extended to cover and govern taste, behaviour, etiquette, language, business deals and politics. It has become a way of life, and is virtually an eleventh commandment for Italians: 'thou shalt give a beguiling outward impression in all that you do in this world'.

Italians have always worshipped beauty, and throughout the centuries have led the world in art and culture, in painting, sculpture, architecture, design and fashion. Today, in a personal sense, Italians seek beauty for themselves, toning their bodies so that they can look their best at all times, and indeed at any cost. Although we may have a generalised inner picture of plump Roman *matrone* and chubby tenors, most Italians these days are very conscious of how they look, and gyms, health clubs and medical facilities for 'aesthetic medicine' (plastic surgery to you and me) are proliferating.

Food to the Italians is not, however, about looking good; it has always been about tasting good, and giving the maximum satisfaction to the palate, about eating for pleasure. Serving a huge spread at parties, with truffles and porcini, is the modern equivalent of the Ancient Roman *bella figura*, where forbidden delicacies such as larks' tongues were offered.

At the opposite end of the spectrum, Gennaro tells a poignant story about his childhood: apparently Gennaro's mother used to make the family go without much food throughout the week so that she could put on a splendid spread on Sunday. Today, however, the new *bella figura* so far as food is concerned is turning to more controlled, more careful eating: many restaurants now have menus that reflect the desire of their clients to eat less, and instead of a *primi*

(pasta or risotto) and a *secondo piatto* (main course), Italian lunchers are choosing steamed vegetables, green salads and yoghurt. It is said that Italians are now amongst the slimmest people in Europe.

Everyone the world over wants to make a good impression on others, but the idea has become extraordinarily ingrained in the Italian consciousness. This might be the result of Italy's history: for a long time the regions now merged into the country were subjected to successive foreign conquests, and years of hardship. I think *la bella figura* evolved as a form of protective armour, an assertion of individuality in the face of an uncomfortable reality. Put on a show so that no-one ever gets to see or understand the real you.

In its more positive aspects *la bella figura* is an expression of personal and national pride. In its more negative aspects, '*la bella figura*' reveals a rather sad superficiality: for instance, many people who flock to Portofino – the billionaire resort of the Ligurian Riviera – do so because they want to pretend, and often have to mortgage themselves to hire the finest car or yacht to feed their fantasies. In a similar vein Italy's erstwhile prime minister, a laughing stock to the rest of Europe, did not embarrass most Italians: his flamboyance kept the country on the world stage. Such behaviour could be said to be the very essence of *la bella figura*, which is basically all about showing off...

Carluccio

500g Italian **'00' flour**, plus extra for dusting
25g **fresh yeast**
450ml lukewarm **water**
salt
2 tbsp **olive oil,** plus extra for greasing

TOPPING
6 tbsp **olive oil**
700g **onions**, finely sliced
1 tbsp **caster sugar**
1 tsp **white wine vinegar**
30 **anchovy fillets**
8 **cherry tomatoes**, halved
freshly ground **black pepper**

SERVES 4–6

Carluccio

Sardenaira
TOMATO, ONION AND ANCHOVY TART

Also called pizza all'Andrea *(after Andrea Doria, the famous Ligurian sailor),* pissadella *or* pissaladeira, *this Ligurian dish reminds me very much of the Provençal* pissaladière, *with only a few small differences. (Provence is not far from Liguria, and at one time the two provinces were connected politically.) It is excellent as a snack, but you could also serve it as a main course with some salad on the side.*

To make the dough, put the flour in a heap on a work surface and make a well in the centre. Dilute the fresh yeast in the water and gradually pour into the well. Add a pinch of salt, and mix well until you have a smooth dough. Cover with a cloth and leave to rise for 4–5 hours.

Meanwhile, make the topping. Heat the olive oil in a large frying pan, and cook the onions until very soft and slightly coloured, about 20 minutes. Add the sugar and vinegar and allow to cook together for another 5 or so minutes.

Preheat the oven to 220°C/Gas 7.

When the dough has risen, knock it back and place on a large oiled baking tray. Press the dough out to form a square, about 2.5cm deep. Cover the surface with the fried onions. Decorate in squares with the anchovy fillets, putting half a tomato in each square. Season with black pepper and drizzle with the olive oil.

Bake in the preheated oven for 20 minutes. Eat hot or warm.

1kg **plain white flour**, plus extra for dusting
500ml **water**
100ml **olive oil**, plus extra for greasing and drizzling
10g **fresh yeast**
20g **salt**
500g *Stracchino* or **Taleggio cheese**

SERVES 4

Carluccio

Focaccia di Formaggio
CHEESE FOCACCIA

With its thin crust and generous filling of cheese, this is a delicious snack to eat at any time of the day. It is the speciality of Camogli, a seaside village in Liguria. The name of the village comes from the local dialect words for 'the houses of the wives'. At one time, the entire male population of the village would have spent most of their time at sea fishing, leaving their wives on land. It is also said that because the men had more than enough fish when away, they were keen on land-based foods like cheese and bread when they came home. The cheese used locally for this dish is Certosino, which is very soft, but I suggest you substitute Stracchino or Taleggio which are more widely available.

Place the flour in a large bowl, and make a well in the centre. Add the water, olive oil, yeast and salt and mix together to form a rough dough. Knead by hand for about 20 minutes (or in a mixer for 5), until the dough is smooth and elastic. Cover with a cloth and leave to rise in a warm place for 30 minutes.

Preheat the oven to 240°C/Gas 9.

Grease a large baking tray with oil. Take half of the dough and on a lightly floured work surface, roll it out with a rolling pin. Then stretch the dough by hand to a thickness of about 3mm. Place on the greased tray and dot with knobs of the cheese.

Roll the other half of the dough out similarly, to the same size and thickness. Place over the cheese, pressing down with your fingers. Seal the edges by pressing, and drizzle some olive oil over the top.

Bake in the very hot oven for 15 minutes or until the focaccia is crisp. Eat immediately, but be careful, the cheese is very hot!

400g **country bread** or *fresella*
  (ready-baked bread)
400g **baby vine tomatoes**, halved
2 tbsp **capers**
16 **green olives**
6 tbsp **extra virgin olive oil**
salt
pinch of **oregano**

SERVES 4

CONTALDO

Pane Caliatu
AEOLIAN BREAD AND CAPER SALAD

I first had this simple salad on the island of Lipari, which produces some of the best capers in Italy. I was amazed at its simplicity: the delicious combination of good local tomatoes, capers and bread. The Sicilian word caliatu *means 'left in the oven': after the bread has been baked once it is re-baked on a very low heat overnight until it has a hard texture. Traditionally this was done so that it lasted longer and I suppose it was used to add texture to salad, originally made with lots of olive oil and whatever local ingredients were seasonally available. In time the recipe has evolved to include potatoes, onions, cucumber and salad leaves – I have kept it simple here though, just as I had it in Lipari.*

If you are using country bread, cut it into slices or chunks and place in the oven on the lowest heat for 2 hours until it has hardened and has a biscuit-type texture. Remove, leave to cool slightly, then drizzle with a little hot water to soften it slightly. If you are using *fresella*, soften with a little water without cooking.

Arrange the bread on a plate with the tomatoes, capers and olives. Drizzle with oil, and sprinkle over the oregano and some salt. Toss well to combine, leave for 10 minutes for the flavours to develop and serve.

500g fresh **porcini** (ceps)
50g **unsalted butter**
2 tbsp **olive oil**
2 **garlic cloves**, sliced
2 tbsp chopped **flat-leaf parsley**
1 tbsp chopped **marjoram leaves**
salt and freshly ground **black
  pepper**

SERVES 4

Carluccio

Funzi ä Funzetto

SAUTÉED MUSHROOMS

*Funzi ä funzetto is Genovese dialect, but you can find a dish of this
nature along all the coasts of the Italian boot. In season, the forests
of the Apennines, rising up not far from the coast, are full of wild
mushrooms. You can eat this dish with toast, scrambled egg, pasta,
rice, or as a side dish for meat or fish. It is simply wonderful.*

Clean the porcini well with a damp cloth, but do not wash them. Slice
them finely.

Melt the butter and oil together in a large frying pan and fry the garlic
gently for a few seconds. Add the porcini and cook, stirring, for 5–6
minutes. Add the herbs and season to taste with salt and pepper.

Eat straightaway.

4 tbsp **extra virgin olive oil**, plus
   extra for drizzling
3 **tomatoes**, sliced
3 **courgettes**, sliced
salt and freshly ground **black
   pepper**
a few **basil leaves**, roughly torn
20g **Parmesan**, freshly grated

SERVES 4

Zucchini e Pomodori al Forno
BAKED COURGETTES AND TOMATOES

*This quick and simple dish – made from vegetables typical of
the warmer south – takes minutes to prepare. It makes an ideal
accompaniment to meat dishes and can even be served by itself
with lots of bread.*

Preheat the oven to 200°C/Gas 6.

Drizzle 2 tablespoons of the oil into an ovenproof dish. Arrange
alternate slices of tomatoes and courgettes in the dish so that they
overlap. Season with salt and pepper, drizzle with the remaining oil,
scatter over the basil leaves and top with the Parmesan.

Bake in the oven for 10 minutes until golden. Remove, drizzle with
some more oil and serve.

Courgettes CONTALDO

Widely used in Italian cooking, the
easy-to-grow courgette is cultivated all
over Italy in different sizes and shades of
green and yellow. Although available all
year round, they are at their best during
spring and early summer. Courgettes can
be boiled and dressed with olive oil and
lemon juice; sautéed in pasta sauces; used
in risotto; stuffed and baked; served *alla
parmigiana*; used in soup; fried in a light
batter or consumed raw in salads. Even
the courgette flowers are used in Italy;
they should be consumed the day they
are picked/bought, filled with ricotta and
deep-fried, or added to soups, risotto
and pasta dishes.

Carciofi Ripieni con Patate
FILLED GLOBE ARTICHOKES WITH POTATOES

When I was a child, street vendors selling roasted artichokes were a common sight: the village would be covered in a haze of smoke, but the aroma was irresistible! One of my favourite ways to cook artichokes is to fill them with all my favourite 'southern' ingredients. The idea of cooking them with potatoes is basically so the artichokes won't wobble in the saucepan, but actually they are really delicious to eat together. Make sure to provide finger bowls when serving (the best way to eat the artichoke leaves is with your hands) and spare plates for the discarded leaves.

First prepare the artichokes. Remove the outer leaves and cut off the stalk. Trim the base slightly so the bottom is flat and the artichoke can stand upright. With your fingers, gently open out the artichoke until you can see the hairy choke. With a small scoop or teaspoon, remove and discard the choke. Season the artichoke cavities with salt and pepper and fill each with: some parsley, 1 sliced garlic clove, 2 anchovies, 6 tomatoes, 1 teaspoon of capers and 2 olives. Gently press all the ingredients in.

Place the filled artichokes in a large saucepan. Pour one tablespoon of oil into each artichoke and cover with any remaining parsley. Place the potatoes in between the gaps. Pour over the vegetable stock, which should come to about ¾ of the way up the artichokes.

Bring to the boil, reduce the heat, cover with a lid and simmer for 1 hour or until the artichokes are tender – test by pulling out a central leaf, if it comes out easily, they are done.

Carefully lift out the artichokes with a large slotted spoon and place on individual serving plates. Gently open them up, pour over a little of the stock and serve with the potatoes and lots of good bread to dip into the sauce.

4 large **globe artichokes**
salt and freshly ground **black pepper**
a handful of **parsley**, roughly chopped
4 **garlic cloves**, thinly sliced
8 **anchovy fillets**
24 **cherry tomatoes**, quartered
4 tsp **capers**
8 **green olives**, pitted and sliced
4 tbsp **extra virgin olive oil**
4 large **potatoes**
1.5 litres **vegetable stock**

SERVES 4

Artichokes CONTALDO

These strange but beautiful looking vegetables from the thistle family are loved by Italians. They are grown in the winter months, with the majority cultivated in the south. There are different varieties, colours and sizes; mainly Romanesco (large and purple), but also *Brindisino, Catanese, Violeta di Chioggia* and *Spinoso Sardo*. Once the outer leaves and hairy choke are removed, artichokes can be roasted, fried, stewed, stuffed or served raw in a salad. The hearts can be preserved in oil to enjoy as antipasto and there is even an artichoke-based aperitif called *Cynar*! Store trimmed artichokes in acidulated water to prevent them from darkening before use.

Carluccio

Struffoli
DEEP-FRIED DOUGHNUTS

Almost all southern dishes involving sugar or caramelised sugar have Arabic origins. The idea of frying pellets of dough (possibly in lard instead of oil) was probably originally to replace hazelnuts, which are much more expensive. Struffoli *are a speciality of Naples and are eaten mainly at Christmas time, though they are often devoured before the celebrations have even started…*

Put the flour into a large bowl and make a well in the centre. Put the eggs, sugar, lemon and orange zest, vodka and a pinch of salt into the well and gradually mix everything together to make a soft dough. Cover with a cloth and leave to rest for 2–3 hours in a cool place.

Take a little of the dough and roll it with your hands into a sausage shape about 1cm thick. Cut this into little chunks 1cm long. Repeat with the remaining dough. (This takes a little time but is worth it!)

When you are ready, heat some oil in a deep-frying pan to moderately hot. Add the dough chunks in batches and fry until crispy and brown, a few minutes only. Lift out with a perforated scoop and drain on absorbent paper.

To make the sauce, put the honey, sugar, water and tangerine strips into a pan, and heat gently to melt the sugar. Simmer for a few minutes until you have a syrupy consistency. Leave to cool.

When ready to serve, pile the *struffoli* up on a serving platter. Pour the syrup over the top, and sprinkle with the candied citron peel to finish.

500g Italian '00' flour
5 eggs
4 tbsp caster sugar
finely grated zest of 1 lemon
finely grated zest of 1 orange
2 tbsp vodka, or whisky
salt
olive oil or lard, for deep-frying
100g candied citron peel, cut into small cubes

SAUCE
250g runny honey
100g caster sugar
2 tbsp water
tangerine peel, cut into fine julienne strips

MAKES 10–12

Citrus Fruits CONTALDO
Introduced by the Arabs to Sicily, citrus fruits have become an integral part of Italian cooking. Oranges are often used with smoked fish or in salads, giving a unique and almost un-Italian flavour! I grew up with the famed lemons from the Amalfi coast, and to me they are as vital in the kitchen as they are for medicinal purposes; I carry a lemon with me wherever I go. Lemons are used to marinate meat and fish, in ice-creams and cakes and are used to make limoncello. Other citrus fruit such as grapefruits are mostly eaten fresh. The fruit and peel are also candied for confectionery purposes.

200g **raspberries**
85g **sugar**
3 **egg yolks**
150ml **milk**
100ml **double cream**
grated zest of 1 **lemon**

SERVES 4

Gelato ai lamponi e limone
RASPBERRY AND LEMON ICE CREAM

Whenever I think of the Italian coast, holidays – and images of strolling along the passegiata *(seafront) with ice-cream cones in hand – inevitably come to mind! I have to admit some of the best ice-creams are Italian, and the flavours you get these days can be quite unusual. I prefer to stick to traditional tastes, and couldn't resist combining some summery raspberries with my beloved Amalfi lemons – though you can make these with strawberries, blueberries, blackberries or a combination, if you prefer.*

Place a suitable empty plastic container in the freezer. Blend half of the raspberries until smooth and mix in 10g of the sugar. Set aside.

Whisk the egg yolks and remaining sugar in a bowl until creamy and the sugar has dissolved. Place the milk and cream in a pan and gently heat through. Remove from the heat and add the egg mixture. Return to a low heat and cook for about a minute, stirring all the time with a wooden spoon, until slightly thickened. Remove from the heat, fold in the raspberry puree, lemon zest and remaining whole raspberries.

Remove the container from the freezer and pour the mixture into it until about ¾ full (any extra should be placed in a separate container). Leave to cool slightly, then place, uncovered, in the freezer. After 30 minutes, remove and stir well, then return to the freezer. Leave for another 30 minutes and repeat this procedure a few times until the ice cream is frozen. Leave in the freezer and use when required. If you have an ice cream machine, churn the mixture until it thickens, then place in a container and freeze, following the manufacturer's instructions.

500g **mulberries** or other fruit like blackberries, raspberries or strawberries
500g **caster sugar**
1.5 litres **water**
juice of 1 **lemon**

MAKES 1.5 LITRES

Carluccio

Granita di Gelsi
MULBERRY GRANITA

I first encountered this granita on the lovely volcanic island of Pantelleria (where some of the best Italian capers come from). Every day, as one does on holiday, I ate at a little local trattoria, where the owner was making this delicious granita from abundant fresh mulberries. (There are many mulberry trees throughout Italy, particularly in the north – the remnants of a once-flourishing silk industry.) The granita is very simple, and very delicious. If you can't get hold of mulberries, try substituting other fruit instead.

Put half the fruit in a large saucepan or preserving pan and add the sugar and water. Cook gently until the sugar has dissolved and the fruit has collapsed. Leave to cool.

When cool, add the remaining fruit and the lemon juice. Mix well, then put into a plastic container and into the freezer. Stir the mixture after 2–3 hours, and then a few times thereafter in order to break down all the large ice crystals.

When the granita is the right texture – smooth and rough at the same time – spoon it into glasses, and serve. Very greedy people would serve this with a dollop of double cream on top, but I don't…

Tree Fruit *Carluccio*
Italians adore fresh tree fruit of any kind, but it must be ripe, for ripeness means aroma and flavour. Bought on a daily basis, it is usually served for dessert. We have a great choice throughout the year: apricots, cherries, citrus, persimmons, medlars, kiwi, quince, mulberries, apples, pears, plums and pomegranates. When I was a child, my job was to find the freshest fruit for dessert: I became quite an expert! In the winter many fruit are served in compotes, baked or encased in pastry. Italian mothers and grandmothers use the best and ripest fruit to produce preserves like jams and jellies.

THE LARDER
of the rivers and plains

MOST OF ITALY'S PLAINS ARE COASTAL, NARROW SLOPES BETWEEN SEA AND MOUNTAIN. On these, as much as possible is cultivated – terraced citrus orchards in Amalfi, serried rows of grape vines at impossible angles, basil on every balcony in Liguria. But many plains are larger, sometimes owing their existence to the presence of a river, which carves its way down to the sea, often leaving alluvial deposits which fortify and fertilise the land. The combination of land and abundant water is something no-one wanting to grow and raise food could resist, and the Italians are no different.

The largest such plain in Italy is that of the Po Valley, the Pianura Padana. The Po, the longest river in Italy, rises in the Alps in the far west and flows east towards the Golfo di Venezia, spreading out into a wide delta. This vast area, a declared natural park with its own unique ecosystem, is surrounded by canals, ancient woods and marshland, and is home to an incredible variety of fish and birds, as well as age-old riverside and lagoon villages. Here life means water, and water has had to transform itself into food. Historically conditions were harsh in the area and its inhabitants had to work extremely hard to survive.

Because of the valley's watery nature – controlled now by irrigation – this is where Italy's rice is cultivated. On drier, often reclaimed land, much of the country's grain is produced – wheat for bread and pasta, maize for polenta, and buckwheat. Vegetables are grown everywhere, as are temperate fruits, and chicken, duck, cattle, sheep and pigs are all bred for eating or preserving in some way, or for producing milk and cheese. Vegetables make up a good proportion of the diet of the locals, and a large variety of greens grow on the embankments. It is not uncommon, still today, to see women collecting basketfuls of wild rocket, endive, radicchio and chard to go into salads and filled pasta. But here the pumpkin is king: the fertile, marshy terrain is ideal for its growth, and the succulent, fleshy interior is used in the renowned *tortelli di zucca* (pumpkin ravioli), as well as in meat dishes, risotto and cakes.

And, of course, there is the wild bounty of the regions – freshwater fish like perch, frogs (which adorn many a northern risotto), mussels, clams, crabs and other shellfish from saltier water in the Veneto. The humid, salty conditions of the Po delta makes an ideal breeding ground for eels, which have provided the area of Comacchio with a lucrative business. There they cook and pickle eels in vinegar, for the home and export market, and this has now been recognised by Slow Food.

Further south, Tuscany and Umbria are more hilly than flat, but in the wonderfully fertile soil of their coastal lowlands grow olive trees, grape vines, potatoes, onions and tomatoes – and sunflowers for oil. An Umbrian speciality is the delicious lentils that have been grown on the volcanic plains of Monti Sibillini above Castelluccio since the time of the Ancient Romans. Further south still is the hot, dry region of Puglia, known as *il tavoliere* or *il granaio d'Italia* (the 'table' or 'granary' of Italy) because most of it is flat plain, with huge acreages of grains, vegetables and fruit. The grain is mostly durum wheat, from which some of Italy's best pasta and bread are made – Puglian bread is now world-famous. Here too wonderful olive oil is produced from trees that are up to 1,000 years old. Much of the region's vast bounty, fruit and vegetable, is turned into preserves: pickled in vinegar, preserved in oil, made into jam or sun-dried.

CONTALDO

Where I grew up on the Amalfi coast, the small, humble river which powered the local paper mill was full of life – small trout, eels, frogs – and these contributed to our diet; my father made sure we always had eel on the Christmas table! The river irrigated the allotments to produce the best pumpkins, aubergines, peppers, salads and herbs.

In Campania and Lazio there are plains as well, watered by great rivers: the Tiber, for instance, flows through Tuscany, Umbria and Lazio on its way to Rome. Much of this great city's food is grown on what was once the Tiber's flood plain, often on reclaimed river marshes. In Campania the type of farming changes completely: because the pasture is sparser than in the lush northern plains, buffalo and sheep cheeses (mozzarella and pecorino respectively) replace cow's cheeses. Tomatoes grow well here, loving the rich potash soils of the plains in the vicinity of Vesuvius, among them the famous San Marzano. Lemon groves abound on the Amalfi coast, and an astonishing array of fruit, nuts and vegetables is grown.

Calabria in the extreme south has a high plain, that of the Sila: the fertile soil of the area produces fruit, vegetables (among them broccoli, its alternate name being 'calabrese'), figs and chestnuts, with a plentitude of wild fungi among the trees. There is even some rice produced here, watered by the rivers descending from the mountains. The southern islands have plains too. Citrus fruit and grape vines flourish around Catania in Sicily, and the volcanic earth at the foot of Mount Etna is the only place in Italy where pistachio nuts can be grown.

2 tbsp **extra virgin olive oil**, plus extra for drizzling

1 **onion**, finely chopped

6 **cherry tomatoes**, halved

2 **fennel bulbs**, trimmed and cut lengthways

120g **spinach leaves**

500g fresh or frozen **broad beans**

2 **potatoes**, cubed

1 litre **vegetable stock**

salt and freshly ground **black pepper**

freshly grated **Parmesan** or pecorino, to serve (optional)

SERVES 4

CONTALDO

Zuppa dell'Orto
GARDEN SOUP

This soup is spring in a bowl. It is made with all the lovely green vegetables which pop up in plains, fields and gardens at this special time of year: the first sweet broad beans, fennel with its fresh aroma and young tender spinach leaves. When produce is as fresh as this, there is little else you need.

Heat the oil in a large saucepan, add the onion and sweat until soft. Stir in the tomatoes. Add the fennel, spinach, broad beans, potatoes and stock. Bring to the boil, lower the heat and simmer, covered, for 25 minutes until the vegetables are tender but not mushy. Remove from the heat, season with salt and pepper and drizzle with oil.

Grate over a little fresh Parmesan or pecorino, if you like, and serve with some good country bread.

4 tbsp **extra virgin olive oil**
1 **onion,** finely chopped
400g **potatoes,** cubed
4 **cherry tomatoes,** quartered
200g **arborio risotto rice**
1.5 litres **vegetable stock**
salt and freshly ground **black pepper**
a handful of **parsley,** finely chopped

SERVES 4

CONTALDO

Zuppa di Riso e Patate
RICE AND POTATO SOUP

This is halfway between a soup and risotto, and I leave it to you as to how you prefer to serve it: at the end of the cooking time, you may add more liquid for a soupier consistency or leave it to rest for 5 minutes for the rice to absorb the liquid. My mother would often make a similar version and as a child it was one of my favourite things to eat. Quick, easy and economical, it makes a perfect midweek meal.

Heat the oil in a saucepan, add the onion and sweat over a medium heat for a couple of minutes. Add the potatoes and tomatoes and cook for a further 2 minutes. Stir in the rice, making sure each grain is coated in the oil. Add the stock and simmer for about 20 minutes until the rice is *al dente* and the potatoes tender. Check from time to time during cooking, adding more hot stock if the rice has absorbed it all. Remove from the heat, season with salt and pepper and stir in the parsley. Serve immediately.

6 tbsp **olive oil**
900g **red and yellow peppers**, cut
  into strips
3 **garlic cloves**, sliced
2 tbsp **white wine vinegar**
12 **eggs**
salt and freshly ground **black
  pepper**

SERVES 4–6

Carluccio

Frittata di Peperoni
SWEET PEPPER OMELETTE

*This is one of the dishes that most reminds me of my youth and my
mother's cooking – it was a regular at picnics. The most important
thing here is to cook the peppers first to achieve a more intense
flavour. The sweet peppers, cooked like this but without the egg,
can also serve as a side dish.*

Heat 5 tablespoons of the oil in a 25cm frying pan and fry the pepper
strips, stirring from time to time, until the edges of the strips are
caramelised, about 10 minutes. Add the garlic and fry gently until it
is cooked but not burnt. Add the vinegar, and cook until evaporated.
Remove from the heat, leaving the peppers in the pan.

Beat the eggs in a bowl and season with salt and pepper.

Return the pepper frying pan to the heat, add the remaining oil
and pour in the egg mixture. Cook, stirring a little with a spatula,
until there is a crust on one side, about 5 minutes. With the help
of a large plate or the lid of a large saucepan, invert the frittata.
Slide it back into the frying pan, crust-side up. Cook for a further
5 minutes, until the other side has browned. Cut into wedges and
serve hot or cold with salad.

4 tbsp **extra virgin olive oil**
1 **shallot**, finely chopped
½ glass **white wine**
200g **cherry tomatoes**, halved
a handful of **dill**, roughly
   chopped
salt and freshly ground **black
   pepper**
350g **linguine**
200g **smoked trout**, roughly
   chopped

SERVES 4

Linguine con Trota Affumicata
LINGUINE WITH SMOKED TROUT AND FRESH DILL

This is a quick and easy pasta dish to make because it uses ready-smoked trout. Cream is usually added to smoked fish when cooking but, as I wanted to keep this light, I have added the freshness of cherry tomatoes instead.

Heat the oil in a frying pan, add the shallot and sweat on a medium heat until softened. Increase the heat, add the wine and allow to evaporate. Stir in the tomatoes and half of the dill and season with salt and pepper. Reduce the heat to low, cover with a lid and leave to gently simmer for 10 minutes. Add the smoked trout to the sauce, stir through and continue to cook for a couple of minutes.

Meanwhile, cook the linguine in plenty of lightly salted boiling water until *al dente*. Drain the pasta, reserving a couple of tablespoons of the cooking water. Stir the pasta and cooking water into the sauce and mix together well. Remove from the heat, sprinkle with the remaining dill and serve immediately.

Lasagne Emiliane
LASAGNE

So many bad versions of lasagne can now be found in fast food restaurants and supermarkets that its reputation seems to have suffered. This is a shame because, if made properly, lasagne really is delicious comfort food at its best. This is my version of the baked pasta dish from Emilia-Romagna, made with the typical Bolognese sauce of the region as well as egg pasta. I have used dried lasagne sheets, which I always keep in my store-cupboard, but you can use the fresh ones readily available in supermarkets or home-made if you prefer (though note that they will need less cooking time).

Heat the oil in a large pan, add the onion and carrot and sweat for a couple of minutes. Add the meats and brown all over. Season with salt. Add the chopped tomatoes and water, lower the heat, cover with a lid and simmer gently for 2 hours, stirring from time to time.

Preheat the oven to 200°C/Gas 6.

To make the white sauce, melt the butter in a small pan on a medium heat. Stir in the flour with either a wooden spoon or small hand whisk to form a paste and stir in a little of the milk. Add the remaining milk gradually, stirring all the time, until it begins to thicken to a creamy consistency. Remove from the heat, add the Parmesan and season with salt and pepper.

Line a 22 x 26cm rectangular ovenproof dish with a little of the Bolognese. Arrange sheets of lasagne over the top, then more Bolognese, a bit of white sauce and some grated Parmesan. Continue to make layers like this until you have finished all the ingredients ending with a topping of white sauce and sprinkled Parmesan.

Cook in the oven for about 35–40 minutes until golden-brown. Remove, leave to rest for a couple of minutes and serve.

2 tbsp **extra virgin olive oil**
1 small **onion**, finely chopped
1 small **carrot**, finely chopped
300g **minced beef**
300g **minced pork**
salt and freshly ground **black pepper**
1 x 400g tin chopped **plum tomatoes** plus the water from rinsing out the tin
8–10 sheets of **dried egg lasagne**
80g **Parmesan**, freshly grated

WHITE SAUCE
60g **butter**
40g **plain flour**
500ml **milk**
20g **Parmesan**, freshly grated

SERVES 4

400g *bucatini*
80g **pecorino**, freshly grated

SAUCE
130g *guanciale*, cut into small cubes
1 small **onion**, finely chopped
3–4 tbsp **extra virgin olive oil**
1 hot dried **red chilli**, finely chopped
2 tbsp **dry white wine**
500g **San Marzano tomatoes**, cut into quarters

SERVES 4

Carluccio

Bucatini all' Amatriciana
PASTA WITH A CHILLI, BACON AND TOMATO SAUCE

This recipe – which originated in Amatrice, near Rome – was taken to heart by Roman chefs and has now become familiar all over the world. It is simplicity itself to make, but you must use bucatino – *a large spaghetti-type pasta with a hole in the middle, which makes it easy to cook. You should also use* guanciale, *cured pig cheek, although you could substitute the less tasty pancetta. Use pecorino cheese here rather than the posher (and dearer) Parmesan.*

For the sauce, put the *guanciale* and onion in a pan with the oil and chilli, and fry gently for about 4–5 minutes. Add the white wine and tomatoes and cook for a further 15–20 minutes, stirring occasionally.

Meanwhile, bring a large saucepan of lightly salted water to the boil, and cook the pasta until *al dente*. Strain the *bucatini* and mix with the sauce. Serve sprinkled generously with the freshly grated pecorino.

Italian Childhood

'OH TO BE A COW IN INDIA, A CAT IN ENGLAND, A CHILD IN ITALY!'
– this saying says it all! Italian children have always come first; they are
put on a pedestal and are almost worshipped. This probably stems back to
religious beliefs that children are a gift from God. In Italian tradition, a child
is a part of you, and therefore the future, so they must be taken care of in
the best possible way. One vital way to ensure this is the case is with the food
given to children, and traditionally kids in Italy eat well, whatever their socio-
economic background.

A typical Italian child's day begins with a breakfast of warm milk with pieces
of bread or nutritious cereal biscuits dipped in. This was my usual breakfast
as a child, though sometimes my mother would make me a milky *zabaglione*
with fresh egg yolk and I would drink it down in one. A favourite time for
children in Italy is *la merenda* – after-school snack time. Traditionally this
is a slice of home-made *crostata di marmellata* (jam tart) a *ciambella* (cake)
or *pane e salame* (salami sandwich), with a glass of milk or *cioccolata calda*
(hot chocolate). As treats, Italian children are given ice-cream, cakes from
the *pasticcerie* (pastry shops), savoiardi biscuits, chocolate eggs at Easter, and
beautifully wrapped traditional sweets in all sorts of natural flavours.

It is quite normal for children in Italy to eat at the table with their parents,
even if this means staying up a little later in the evening. In most families
the table will be laid properly and there will be bread, water and wine for
the adults, with perhaps a thimbleful of wine mixed with water for the
children. Wine is considered very much part of the Italian meal and a good
digestion aid. In general children tend to eat whatever their parents eat, and
in traditional families the typical Italian three-course meal of pasta or risotto,
main course and fruit is the norm. As a result, Italian children grow up with a
knowledge of food, and talking about what they had for dinner last night is a
perfectly normal conversation amongst primary-school children!

There are lots of myths about what can or cannot be given to children
and even at what time. For instance, I remember my mother saying that
bananas should never be eaten before bedtime as they are heavy to digest,
and oranges, too, because of their high content of acidity, would give you a
sleepless night. On Italian beaches throughout the summer, children have to
wait a full two hours after breakfast before they are allowed to go swimming.
These beliefs are handed down from generation to generation, and I still hear
Italian mothers issuing such warnings to their children. Yet for many Italians,
childhood is the best time of their life: years of carelessness, discovery, growth,

family life, mamma's comfort food and reassurance, games and adventures with friends. Hardships are kept hidden from the children as much as possible, and for those who struggle financially, sacrifices are made so that their precious offspring don't go without.

However, there is a downside to this over-protection. Traditionally *la mamma* stayed at home and spent a vast majority of her time and energy on the children in an almost obsessive manner. It is a well-known fact that Italian boys are their mother's 'darlings'. Many have been so pampered and, in their mother's eyes, can do no wrong, that as adults, they have actually never really matured psychologically. It is not unusual for thirty- to forty-year-old Italian men to be still living at home. Known as *mammoni*, and 'undetached from mamma', these men rarely contribute financially, or help in the home (let alone cook) as mamma is quite happy to do all this for them.

Times are changing, as in all modern societies, and with the influx of fast-food chains, convenience food and a more sedentary lifestyle, Italian children are perhaps not eating as well or getting as much exercise as they used to. From what we have seen though, this tends to be mostly in large towns and cities in the north of Italy. In smaller, rural towns and villages, and in the south, traditions still apply, and only the best, freshest ingredients are bought to feed the whole family.

CONTALDO

1.5 litres **vegetable stock**
3 tbsp **extra virgin olive oil**
1 small **onion**, finely chopped
½ **celery stalk**, finely chopped
¼ fresh **red chilli**, finely chopped
  (optional)
1 sprig of **rosemary**
300g **arborio risotto rice**
60ml **white wine**
300g **pumpkin**, cubed
40g **unsalted butter**
60g **Parmesan**, freshly grated,
  plus extra to serve

SERVES 4

Risotto alla Zucca
PUMPKIN RISOTTO

Varieties of pumpkin are grown all over Italy, especially on the northern plains, where rice is grown as well. Pumpkin was originally a food of the poor and was traditionally eaten by farmers. Now pumpkin risotto is a popular dish, especially in rice-producing Lombardy in autumn, when this vegetable is plentiful and at its best. Growing up in southern Italy I always enjoyed eating pumpkin at home with pasta; it was only on trips to northern Italy later that I discovered this wonderful combination.

Put the stock in a saucepan and bring to a gentle simmer. Leave over a low heat.

Heat the oil in a saucepan, and sweat the onion, celery, chilli and rosemary until the vegetables soften. Add the rice and stir well, making sure each grain is coated in the oil. Add the wine and keep stirring until it evaporates. Add the pumpkin together with a ladle of stock and cook, stirring all the time, until the stock has been absorbed. Add another ladle of stock and repeat. Continue to do this for about 20 minutes until the rice is *al dente*.

Remove from the heat and stir in the butter and Parmesan. Divide between four bowls, sprinkle over a little more Parmesan and serve.

3 tbsp **extra virgin olive oil**
1 small **onion**, finely chopped
150g **minced pork**
200g **pearl barley**
120g **spinach**, roughly chopped
½ glass **white wine**
1 litre **vegetable stock**
a handful of **flat-leaf parsley**,
  finely chopped
freshly ground **black pepper**

SERVES 4

CONTALDO

Orzotto con Spinaci e Macinato di Maiale
PEARL BARLEY WITH SPINACH AND PORK MINCE

The ancient grain of orzo perlato, *pearl barley, is able to grow almost anywhere – from temperate coastal plains and tropical highlands, to sub-Saharan Africa and the sub-Arctic. In Italy it is grown in the cooler mountain regions as well as on the plains from the north to the south. Pearl barley is a great substitute for rice: in fact, not only does this dish look like risotto when finished, it is actually cooked in the same way. This simple-to-prepare dish makes a complete and nourishing meal.*

Heat 1 tablespoon of the oil in a large saucepan, add the onion and pork and cook, stirring, until the onion is soft and the pork sealed. Stir in the pearl barley and spinach and cook for a couple of minutes. Add the white wine and allow to evaporate. Now gradually add the stock ladle by ladle, waiting until each ladleful has been absorbed before you add the next. Continue until the pearl barley is cooked, about 30 minutes.

Remove from the heat, mix in the remaining oil and parsley and season with black pepper. Serve immediately.

4 **perch** (or trout, tench or carp),
    about 200g each, gutted and
    fins removed
plain flour, for coating
salt and freshly ground **black
    pepper**
100ml **olive oil**
100g **unsalted butter**
2 tbsp finely chopped **flat-leaf
    parsley**
1 tbsp **wild thyme leaves**
4 **eggs**
150ml **white wine vinegar**

SERVES 4

Carluccio

Pesce Persico in Carpione d'Uovo
MARINATED PERCH WITH EGG

There are many 'in carpione' recipes in Italy, especially in areas where sweet freshwater fish are available. This one, from Lake Como, is quite unusual because of the egg – which takes away some of the 'muddy' taste many people dislike in such fish.

Dust the fish with flour both inside and out, and season with salt and pepper.

Heat half of the olive oil and butter together in a large frying pan, add the fish and cook on both sides until golden, about 10 minutes. Drain on kitchen paper and place on a glass or china serving dish.

Clean the pan out with kitchen paper, and melt the remaining oil and butter. Fry the parsley and thyme leaves gently for a few minutes.

Meanwhile, beat the eggs in a large bowl with some salt and pepper. Whisk in the vinegar. Pour this into the frying pan and heat very gently for a minute or two: you don't want the eggs to coagulate, they must still be liquid. Pour this vinegar mixture over the fish and leave overnight. Eat cold as an antipasto or with some polenta (see page 39) as a main course.

CONTALDO

Luccio Tonnato
PIKE IN A TANGY TUNA SAUCE

Pike is a typical freshwater fish found in rivers all over Italy. It is quite bony, so I would ask your fishmonger for fillets instead of buying whole. If you are unable to find pike, a good substitute is best-quality organic salmon. This sauce, particularly popular in Piedmont, is traditionally served with cold slices of veal – however it marries really well with pike and makes a perfect summer dish. It can be made the day before and stored in the fridge until required.

Place the pike fillets in a saucepan with the vinegar, bay leaves, peppercorns and enough water to cover. Bring to the boil, lower the heat and simmer gently for about 8–10 minutes until cooked.

Meanwhile combine all the sauce ingredients in a food processor and blend to obtain a creamy consistency.

Drain the cooked pike and leave to cool. Arrange on a plate, pour over the sauce and leave in the fridge for at least 4 hours before serving.

1kg **pike** (or salmon) **fillets**
1 glass **white wine vinegar**
2 **bay leaves**
10 **black peppercorns**

SAUCE
2 x 185g tins **tuna** in oil, drained
25g **capers**
6 **anchovy fillets**
a handful of **parsley**
250ml **olive oil**

SERVES 4–6

4 **whole trout**, about 450g each, gutted, cleaned and scaled

50g **hazelnuts**

50g **almonds**

40g **pine nuts**

8 **anchovy fillets**

3 **garlic cloves**

2 tbsp **capers**

2 **eggs**, beaten

50g *grissini* (breadsticks), crushed

a handful of **parsley**, finely chopped

40g **Parmesan**, freshly grated

grated zest of 1 **lemon**

salt and freshly ground **black pepper**

extra virgin olive oil, for greasing and drizzling

lemon juice, for drizzling

SERVES 4

CONTALDO

Trote Ripiene al Forno
FILLED BAKED TROUT

This freshwater fish is one of my favourites, not only to eat but to catch: I used to fish for smaller trout in Italian rivers, and now I go fly-fishing in England. Trout can be prepared in many ways, even eaten raw in carpaccio. The filling for this recipe may seem heavy, but the earthy flavours of the nuts combine really well with the fish. Serve with a green salad.

Preheat the oven to 180°C/Gas 6.

Rinse the fish inside and out. Set aside. Place the nuts, anchovies, garlic and capers in a food processor and whiz together. Place in a bowl and stir in the eggs, *grissini*, parsley, Parmesan, lemon zest, salt and pepper until you obtain a paste-like consistency. If it appears too wet, add some more crushed *grissini*.

Fill the cavities of the trout with this mixture. Tie the fish in 3 places with string or raffia. Place the filled trout on a greased ovenproof dish and drizzle a little oil over the top. Make small incisions in the fish skin between the string and bake in the oven for 15–20 minutes, until the fish is cooked through. Remove, drizzle with a little more oil and lemon juice and serve.

2kg medium **eel**, heads off, cleaned and cut into 10cm chunks
plain flour, for coating
salt and freshly ground **black pepper**
150ml **olive oil**
4–5 **garlic cloves**, sliced
6 tbsp **white wine vinegar**
a handful of **mint leaves**

SERVES 4–6

Carluccio

Anguilla alla Scapece
MARINATED EEL

Eel swim thousands of miles from their birthplace in the Sargasso Sea (off the American coast) to the rivers of Europe. In Italy they are found at the mouth of the Po, in the Tiber, and in Sicily and Sardinia. A favourite Roman recipe at Christmas is capitone, *a mature female eel which is cut into chunks, marinated and cured in oil, vinegar and herbs, then grilled over charcoal. Here we are using smaller eels and reversing the process, frying the eel chunks first, then marinating them. Marinated fish are popular in Italy and are usually eaten at the start of the meal as an antipasto.*

Put the chunks of eel in a plastic bag with a bit of flour, salt and pepper. Close with your hand and shake to coat. Remove the eel from the bag, shaking off any surplus flour.

Heat half the oil in a large frying pan. Add the the eel and fry, in batches if necessary, until brown on all sides. Remove from the oil and drain on kitchen paper. Place on a glass or china serving dish.

Remove the oil from the pan and wipe it out with kitchen paper. Add the remaining oil and heat gently. Add the garlic and fry until soft but not browned. Pour in the vinegar, and season with salt and pepper. Leave to cool.

When the oil and vinegar mixture is cool, add the mint leaves. Pour over the eel and leave to marinate for at least 5–6 hours, preferably overnight, turning from time to time. Serve cold.

500g **minced pork**
500g **minced beef**
150g **prosciutto**, finely chopped
30g **dried breadcrumbs**
salt and freshly ground **black pepper**
3 **eggs**
70g **Parmesan**, freshly grated
20g finely chopped **parsley**
pinch of freshly grated **nutmeg**
a little **plain flour**, for dusting
60g **butter**
2 **onions**, roughly chopped
100ml **white wine**
2 **bay leaves**
1.5 litre **milk**

SERVES 6–8

CONTALDO

Polpettone al Latte
MEATLOAF COOKED IN MILK

This traditional meatloaf comes from around Cremona and Mantua in Lombardy, where it is common to slow-cook meat in milk. This unusual way of cooking may stem from the fact that milk was an easy ingredient to come by in rural areas: it also tenderises meat very well. Many recipes call for veal and pork, and some traditionalists will cook the meat for up to 12 hours on a very gentle heat. The polpettone *is delicious eaten hot with a little of the creamy sauce, but is equally good served cold the next day.*

In a large bowl, combine the pork, beef, prosciutto, breadcrumbs, some salt and pepper, eggs, Parmesan, parsley and nutmeg using your hands. When all well amalgamated, divide the mixture into two equal portions and shape each into a large, fat sausage. Lightly dust each *polpettone* with flour all over. Set aside.

In a large saucepan, melt the butter, add the onion and gently fry for about 5 minutes, taking care not to burn it. Remove from the heat and discard the onion by filtering through a fine sieve. Return the melted butter to the pan and return to the heat, add the meat *polpettoni* and seal on all sides – if necessary, add more butter. Add the wine and allow to evaporate. Add the bay leaves and milk and bring to the boil. Reduce the heat to low, cover with a lid and cook for 2 hours. Carefully remove and place on a large plate, slice and serve with the creamy sauce.

1.5kg **boned capon,** or as large a chicken as you can find

1 **onion**

2 **celery stalks**

5 **bay leaves**

2 **carrots**

STUFFING

30 **walnut halves**

1 tbsp **pine kernels**

50ml **single cream**

100g **dried breadcrumbs**

60g **unsalted butter**

3 **egg yolks**

60g **Parmesan,** freshly grated

salt and freshly ground **black pepper**

freshly grated **nutmeg**

5 large **sage leaves,** chopped

1 tbsp **capers,** rinsed

1 tbsp chopped **rosemary**

GREEN SAUCE

1 **bread roll**

 a little **white wine vinegar**

4 tbsp finely chopped **flat-leaf parsley**

2 **cornichons**

1 **garlic clove**

2 **anchovy fillets**

olive oil

SERVES 6–8

Carluccio

Cappone Farcito Bollito in Brodo

STUFFED CAPON BOILED IN BROTH

This dish from Lombardy dates back to the 18th century, though it is still very valued today. Capons (castrated cockerels) are produced, usually for the Christmas market, in the plains of Veneto, Emilia-Romagna, Lombardy and Piedmont. You will probably have to order one specially from your butcher, and you should also ask him to bone it for you. Remember to save the wonderful stock, in which you can cook tortellini or ravioli to serve as a starter. The sauce here is also very good with other boiled meats.

To make the stuffing, put all the ingredients in a bowl and mix together until you have a paste. Stuff the cavity of the capon with this, and if necessary, tie the bird up with string to hold it closed.

Immerse the capon in water in a large saucepan. Add the onion, celery, bay leaves and carrots. Bring to the boil, cover, reduce the heat and simmer for 2 hours.

To make the green sauce, take the breadcrumbs out of the centre of the roll, and soak them in a little vinegar for a few minutes. Squeeze them dry, and put in a bowl with the chopped parsley. Chop the cornichons, garlic and anchovies finely as well, and add to the bowl. Gradually add enough olive oil to make a smooth but not too liquid sauce.

Serve the capon in slices with a little stuffing, and the green sauce. If you have some, accompany with a few *mostarda di Cremona* (mustard-crystallised fruits).

4 large **chicken breasts**, skinned
   and minced
2 **eggs**
3 tbsp **dried breadcrumbs**
2 **garlic cloves**, very finely
   crushed
salt and freshly ground **black
   pepper**
freshly grated **nutmeg**
4 tbsp **olive oil**, for frying
1 x 400g tin chopped **tomatoes**

SERVES 4

Carluccio

Ngozzammoddi
CHICKEN AND TOMATO RISSOLES

I like this dish, born in the ghetto of Rome, primarily because of its simplicity. If you want it to be truly authentic, when buying your chicken breasts, ask your butcher for a piece with the wishbone. Donatella Limentani Pavoncello – whose family have been influential in Rome for some four to five centuries – told me that the wishbone is absolutely essential and has to be given to the most important person at the table…

Mix the chicken mince with the eggs, breadcrumbs, garlic, salt, pepper and nutmeg in a bowl, using your hands. Divide the mixture into eight and shape into ovals.

Heat the oil in a medium frying pan and brown the rissoles on all sides, about 6 minutes. Add the chopped tomatoes, and cook together for another 10 minutes or so. Remove from the heat. Divide the rissoles between plates and serve accompanied with some good bread and a little *broccoletti strascinati* (see opposite), if you like.

Poultry *Carluccio*

When I was growing up in Piedmont we kept chickens, ducks, rabbits and a goat; we had milk and eggs every day, and, occasionally, some meat. This type of animal husbandry is traditional in Italy. Most Italian chickens are free-range, often corn-fed and are a favourite meat. Capons, castrated cockerels, are very popular in Italy and France, especially at Christmas; the Ancient Romans discovered that castration resulted in plumper and meatier birds. In Britain, this practice has been forbidden, but they can be imported from the Continent. Ducks and geese are popular in the north, where they are raised for meat and for *fegato grasso*, the Italian foie gras. Geese and turkeys are eaten at festive times, just as in the UK.

Carluccio

Broccoletti Strascinati

BRAISED RAPE TOPS/BROCCOLI

This simple vegetable dish is common to all the southern regions. Often it is eaten just with bread as an easy snack, but it can also accompany many dishes as a side vegetable. In Rome the vegetables are cooked in lard, which gives a much more interesting flavour, but you can use olive oil instead, if you like.

Trim and wash the vegetables, cutting off the tougher ends of the stem if necessary.

Heat the lard in a large pan with a lid, and fry the chilli and garlic very briefly until soft. Add the rape tops and a little salt and cook for about 7–8 minutes: taste a stalk to check whether it is *al dente* enough for you – should you need to cook them longer just add a little water. Serve immediately.

600g **rape tops** or sprouting broccoli
4 tbsp **lard** (or olive oil)
1 fresh **red chilli**, finely chopped
2 **garlic cloves**, sliced
salt

SERVES 4

Rome and the Romans

Rome, 'the Eternal City', is said in legend to have been founded around 753 BC, by Romulus and Remus, the twin sons of a priestess and Mars, the god of war. Abandoned at birth beside the Tiber river, they were first saved and suckled by a she-wolf, then were later brought up by a local shepherd. When grown, Mars asked them to establish a city near where they were found. In reality, the city probably grew gradually, with people from villages on the surrounding hills moving down to the river valley, where the flat land and fertile soil offered greater scope for animal breeding and agriculture.

From these humble beginnings, the accumulation of villages which became Rome grew to be the most powerful state in history. The Ancient Romans formed a republic and an empire, ruling most of the then known world, spreading their culture and beliefs, their architecture and engineering skills, as well as their foodstuffs. The fall of the Roman power around the late fifth century, is endlessly debated, but the city itself survived, and is now the capital of a united Italy.

Situated on the plain of the Tiber valley, Rome encompasses those seven hills from which its earliest inhabitants probably came, and has stretched over the whole area. The Tiber itself was once the Roman conduit for goods from Carthaginian, Spanish and French ships, and delivered Tuscan and Umbrian trade to the sea. It is now only navigable as far as Rome and, because it was prone to severe flooding, has been contained by massive wall-embankments of travertine limestone (the rock used for part of St Peter's, the Spanish Steps and the Colosseum).

That same flooding, however, along with ancient volcanic residue, has made the soil of the surrounding countryside extremely fertile, and the whole of Lazio (once known as Latium) still serves as a larder for Rome, producing the raw ingredients demanded by the hungry city. Most Roman dishes are based on these seasonally available ingredients, principally vegetables such as peas, globe artichokes and fava or broad beans, as well as garlic, broccoli and *broccoletti* (the Roman name for *cime di rapa*, or rape tops). Wheat is grown too for the many pasta dishes characteristic of Roman cooking, among them *bucatini all'amatriciana*, *spaghetti carbonara*, and *fettuccine* (the Roman version of Emilian tagliatelle) with a number of sauces, which might include *puttanesca*, *cacio e pepe*, *ajo e ojo* and *all'Alfredo*. Semolina flour is used in *gnocchi alla romana*, which are

made in a similar way to *polenta concia*, but are then baked. The best-known cheeses are pecorino romano, caciotta and mozzarella. Ricotta, the soft cheese mostly used in desserts, is a by-product of pecorino-making.

Meat is produced for Rome in the surrounding provinces, principally lamb (milk-fed a particular speciality) and kid. Lamb is braised, baked, grilled, and served *brodettato* – in a stew enriched with egg yolks and lemon juice, served in Rome at Easter. This was an idea 'borrowed' from the Greek tradition: once empire-builders and -takers, the Romans are no different in cookery, and many traditional Roman dishes have been commandeered from neighbouring regions and indeed nearby countries. Pork is popular too, and the dish most associated with Rome and Lazio must be *porchetta*, a suckling pig, boned, marinated with herbs, stuffed and roasted: it can be eaten as a main course or served in slices in a *panino*. *Guanciale*, pork cheek cured in salt then air-dried is perhaps the most famous meat product, and is used in genuine *carbonara* and *amatriciana* pasta sauces.

Other meats enjoyed by Romans are, curiously, beef and veal (a famous Roman dish is *saltimbocca alla romana*) and, I am afraid, donkey and horse meat. The latter are dried for *coppiette* (strips of easy to carry meat for farmers and herdsmen). But the principal passion in Roman meat cooking is offal, for which there are many recipes. Historically Rome's slaughterhouses were based in Testaccio (on the eastern side of the Tiber), and after the prime cuts had been taken by the rich, the less privileged were left with what is known as 'the fifth' quarter of the animal: things like tripe, sweetbreads, brains, and *paiata* or *pagliata* (entrails of milk-fed lamb) which, braised, have today achieved a status of great delicacy and are served in the best restaurants. On our travels, Gennaro and I even tried *testicole di cavallo*, horse testicles, which are mostly eaten by men for fairly obvious reasons...

Roman dishes have their roots firmly in the past, and one of the major influences must be that of the Jewish community. Jews had lived in Rome since before Christian times, but were forced to live in a ghetto – in an insalubrious area liable to flooding – by papal edict in 1555. A few years ago I met Donatella Limentani Pavoncello, whose family can trace their roots back those 500 years, and she said that her family was responsible for that famous Jewish artichoke recipe, *carciofi alla giudia*. Excluded from most professions, the ghetto Jews became *friggitori*, street vendors cooking and selling all sorts of fried foods: fish, meat, liver and lots of vegetables. *The fritto misto* served in expensive restaurants today had its origins in the Roman ghetto and its *friggitori*.

And as for the Romans themselves, they still think they are living in the Roman Empire. That they are the first citizens of Italy is etched into the psyche of every Roman male in particular, which in turn leads to the classic signs of *machismo*. (The term *macho* carries multiple meanings: once it was positive, meaning manly, responsible, courageous; now it is generally more negative, portrayed as hypermasculinity, aggression even).

Many men in Rome display *machismo*, especially where women and football are concerned – but are they real men? Behind the good looks, style and arrogance, are they independent, strong, manly, sexy, generous? They may appear all these things (projecting that sense of *la bella figura*), but machismo often goes hand in hand with a fear of self-reliance, of commitment, of growing up… Some 70 per cent of unmarried Italian men over the age of thirty-five, particularly in Rome, are said to still live at home. Although to our eyes, these are the *mammoni*, the 'mummy's boys' who have not managed to escape their mamma's apron strings, in Rome they are far from objects of derision. For some reason, they are well respected…

Carluccio

500g **swiss chard**
60g **butter**
salt and freshly ground **black pepper**
150ml hot **water**
40g **walnuts**, roughly chopped
40g **Parmesan**, freshly grated

SERVES 4

CONTALDO

Coste al Burro e Parmigiano
SWISS CHARD WITH BUTTER AND PARMESAN

Swiss chard, similar to spinach in appearance, is found growing on the northern plains and marshlands of the Po Delta: why it is known as 'Swiss' no-one seems to know, and it is most highly prized in France and Italy. It is sometimes referred to as erbette *and is used as a popular accompaniment to main courses, and as a filling for the local ravioli and tortelli pastas. The latter is a speciality in Emilia-Romagna for the feast of San Giovanni, when they are enjoyed at home or at the numerous* sagre *(food festivals) around the area.*

Cut off the white stalks of the chard, remove any stringy bits and roughly chop into chunks. Keep the tender green leaves, discarding the tough ones.

Melt the butter in a frying pan, add the white chard stalks and a little salt and sauté for a couple of minutes until slightly golden. Add the hot water, cover with a lid and cook on a medium heat for 10 minutes, stirring from time to time. Add the green leaves, cover with the lid and cook for a further 5 minutes. Stir in the walnuts, Parmesan and pepper. Remove from the heat and serve immediately.

60ml **olive oil**
400g small **green peppers**
salt

SERVES 4

Carluccio

Friarelli
FRIED SMALL GREEN PEPPERS

Friarelli, or peperoni verdi, are small green peppers, which look like chillies, but are not hot. Simply fried in olive oil and eaten seeds and all, they are one of the most typical peasant dishes, especially in the south of Italy. I first encountered them when I saw Puglian farmers putting them in sandwiches for their meal, but I have seen them lately in restaurants where they are served as amusing snacks. Many good supermarkets now sell these peppers.

Wash the peppers, and trim the stalks. Heat the oil in a frying pan over a medium heat, and add the peppers. Fry them for about 10 minutes, stirring often. The skin will be soft, wrinkled and charred (but not burnt) and the seeds tender.

Remove from the pan, arrange on a plate and sprinkle with salt. The little peppers can be eaten as a starter or a side vegetable, though they are particularly good as an interesting snack with an aperitif.

Sweet Peppers
CONTALDO

Brightly coloured and glowing with Mediterranean sunshine, this vegetable is another favourite with Italians. Adding a vibrant green, red, yellow and orange as well as sweetness to dishes, their popularity has spread throughout the Italian regions. They can be grilled, fried and/or used in pasta sauces; made into a Piedmontese *peperonata* (mixed pepper stew); into *agrodolce* (cooked with sweet and sour flavours); stuffed and then baked; as well as eaten raw in salads and preserved in oil as an antipasto. Certain varieties grow only in certain regions: for example, *friarelli* (or *friggitelli*), a small green pepper, is cultivated on the Campanian plains. The peppers from Piedmont, *peperoni di Carmagnola*, are considered the best in Italy.

2 **pears**
2 heads of **radicchio**
150g **walnuts**
120g **Gorgonzola cheese**, cubed
a few strands of **chives**, to garnish

DRESSING
1 small **shallot**, very finely
   chopped
8 tbsp **extra virgin olive oil**
2 tbsp **red wine vinegar**
1 tsp strong **mustard**

SERVES 4

CONTALDO

Insalata di Pere e Gorgonzola
PEAR AND GORGONZOLA SALAD

Gorgonzola is a rich blue cheese from Lombardy, made from the milk of grazing Alpine cows. It combines well with pears, and this dish is often eaten after meals. Radicchio, a reddish-purple salad leaf from the chicory family, grows in the Veneto region. There are two types: the rosso di Verona, *a round ball-like shape found all year round, and my favourite,* radicchio di Treviso, *long and narrow and only available in winter. The combination of soft, sweet pear, creamy Gorgonzola and crunchy walnuts marries perfectly with the slight bitterness of radicchio.*

Core the pears and cut into thin slices. Separate the radicchio leaves and place in a large bowl with the pear slices, walnuts and Gorgonzola.

Combine the dressing ingredients and pour over the salad, tossing well to combine. Garnish with chives and serve.

12–16 *puntarelle* shoots
3 tbsp **olive oil**
juice of 1 **lemon**
3 **anchovy fillets**
salt and freshly ground **black
    pepper**
20 **mint leaves**

SERVES 4

Carluccio

Insalata di Puntarelle alla Menta
CHICORY SALAD WITH MINT

Extremely popular around Rome, puntarelle *is a member of the chicory family, originally descended from a plant very similar to the dandelion. It tastes slightly bitter (something the Italians love) but the texture is very tender. Shoots of chicory grow from a compact head, very tightly packed together – the leaves are removed from the stalks, which are cut into extremely thin strips. These can be eaten cooked as a vegetable, or raw in a salad. It wouldn't be the same, but you could use asparagus prepared in the same way instead.*

Cut the *puntarelle* shoots into thin strips. Place in a salad bowl.

Combine the oil and lemon juice to make a dressing. Mash the anchovy fillets to a paste and add to the dressing with a little salt and lots of black pepper. Mix well.

Pour the dressing over the *puntarelle*. Add the mint leaves, toss together to combine and serve immediately.

Carluccio

Melanzane Ripiene
STUFFED AUBERGINE

The aubergine is a very ancient vegetable which grows particularly well on the warm plains of the south, and Italy has adopted it almost as a national vegetable: you will encounter it all over the place in a number of guises. One of the best ways of cooking it is as a vessel for carrying various other goodies, thus becoming a meal in itself. Needless to say, almost every region, indeed almost every family, has its own particular way of personalising the dish.

Preheat the oven to 220°C/Gas 7. Sprinkle a few drops of olive oil over a baking sheet.

Using a spoon, take the inside flesh of the aubergine halves out of the skin, leaving a casing that is about 1cm thick. Chop the flesh finely. Chop the anchovies, capers and olives finely as well. Mix all these together with the breadcrumbs, tomato and some salt and pepper. (Be careful with the salt, as the anchovies and capers are salty already.)

Put the aubergine skins on the greased baking tray and gently spoon in the stuffing, dividing it equally and trying to keep the natural shape of the vegetable. Sprinkle generously with olive oil, about 1 tablespoon per aubergine half, and bake in the preheated oven for 30 minutes. Serve warm or cold with a simple salad, if you like.

olive oil
2 large **aubergine**s or 4 small, cut in half lengthways
4 **anchovy fillets**
1 tbsp **capers**, soaked in water for 10 minutes, then drained
2 tbsp pitted **black olives**
4 tbsp **fresh breadcrumbs**
4 tbsp fresh chopped **tomatoes** or tinned
salt and freshly ground **black pepper**

SERVES 4

Aubergines CONTALDO
These versatile vegetables are mainly grown in the south. The most popular dish is *parmigiana di melanzane*, fried aubergine slices with tomato sauce, Parmesan and mozzarella. They have an almost 'meat-like' quality to them, which is why poorer housewives made them into *polpette* (meatballs). Aubergines form the basis of many Sicilian sauces and the caponata stew. They can be roasted, grilled and stuffed, and in Amalfi are even dipped into chocolate for dessert! Preserve them raw in oil to enjoy as an antipasto with cured meats and cheese (my favourite!). When frying, be careful as they absorb lots of oil: do not be tempted to add more, simply lower the heat.

1.7 litres **milk**
1 **vanilla pod**
rind of ½ **lemon**
200g **sugar**
300g **arborio rice**
5 large **eggs**, separated
50ml **orange liqueur**
40g **raisins**
grated zest of 1 **orange**, plus extra
    for serving

SERVES 8–10

Torta di Riso al Profumo d'Arancio
ORANGE RICE CAKE

Rice is sometimes used for making cakes in Italy and this is certainly true in the northern regions, where it is cultivated and plentiful. This cake is extremely nutritious and filling – perfect as a teatime snack for children home from school, or even for breakfast!

Preheat the oven to 180°C/Gas 4. Grease and line a 24cm loose-bottomed cake tin with greaseproof paper.

Place the milk, vanilla pod, lemon rind and sugar in a large saucepan and bring to the boil. Add the rice and simmer on a medium to low heat for about 20–25 minutes, until the rice is *al dente* and has absorbed the milk but still has a creamy consistency. Remove from the heat and allow to cool. Discard the lemon rind.

In a bowl, whisk the egg yolks and liqueur until creamy. In another bowl, whisk the egg whites until stiff.

Add the egg yolk mixture to the cooled rice, then fold in the stiffened egg whites, followed by the raisins and orange zest. Pour in the prepared tin and bake in the oven for 1 hour. Serve warm or cold, sprinkled with a little extra orange zest to finish.

Spirits and Liqueurs
Carluccio

Italians love aperitif and digestif spirits, especially the latter. Most of them are commercially bottled – once by monasteries and pharmacies – but some can be made at home. For this you need pure 95 per cent (by volume) alcohol, which you can buy freely in Italy. After maceration with herbs, roots or other flavourings, it is diluted to drinkable strength. (You could use strong vodka or schnapps.) I make *nocino*, with green walnuts and limoncello, and *Sardinian mirto*, made with myrtle. There are many liqueurs called *amaro* (bitter). The brandy of Italy is *grappa*, made from pomace (the pressed grape pulp, skins and stems left over from wine-making) and there are hundreds of varieties. It can be added to a morning espresso, a *caffè corretto* ('corrected coffee').

rice paper, for lining
300g dried figs and dates, pitted
2 tbsp runny honey
50ml Vin Santo
½ tsp each of cloves, cinnamon,
   pepper, nutmeg
3 tbsp plain flour
100g soft brown sugar
300g candied fruit (citron,
   lemon, orange etc)
100g peeled almonds
icing sugar, for dusting

MAKES 800G–1KG

Preserved Fruit and Vegetables CONTALDO

Italians have always loved to preserve food; it is a way of keeping the aroma and flavours of produce long after it is out of season. When I was growing up, our larder was full of aubergines, peppers, courgettes, green beans, artichokes and mushrooms, all preserved in oil. These were excellent as antipasto or in a panini. At the end of summer tomatoes were bottled, sun-dried and made into *concentrato* (a thick purée). Strawberries, plums, peaches and apricots were made into jams or put in syrup; cherries were kept in alcohol; figs were sun-dried. Despite freezers and the ease of finding fresh produce all year round, I still keep up this tradition.

Carluccio

Panforte Senese
TRADITIONAL SIENESE CAKE

This very famous sweet dates back to the 13th century, and is most strongly associated with Siena, in Tuscany. Literally translated as 'strong bread', panforte may have Arabic origins, as it was originally very highly spiced. Today it is made with fewer ingredients, but still has an 'ancient' taste. It is delightful eaten in small morsels, either with tea or at the end of the meal with coffee and liqueurs.

Preheat the oven to 160°C/Gas 3. Line a 25cm round or a 20cm square baking tin with rice paper.

Mince the figs and dates coarsely, then put into a saucepan. Add the honey and cover with the Vin Santo. Add the spices, flour and brown sugar, and melt over a gentle heat until everything comes together. Cook gently for 10 minutes.

Pour the mixture into a bowl and add the candied fruit and almonds. Mix well and pour everything into the lined baking tin. Bake for 40–45 minutes, then remove from the oven and leave to cool. Sprinkle with icing sugar and serve cut into morsels.

Sbriciolata di Pesche

PEACH AND RICOTTA CRUMBLE

This is fruit crumble, Italian-style! The base is a sweet shortcrust pastry and is accompanied by a rich filling of ricotta and peaches and finished with a crumble topping. The Mediterranean climate is ideal for the cultivation of peaches, and Italy has some of the finest varieties. Grown on the plains of Emilia-Romagna, Veneto and Campania, they are one of Italy's best-loved summer fruits. You can replace the peach with other fruit like apricots, plums or mixed berries or even fruit in syrup out of season, if you prefer.

First make the pastry base. Combine all the ingredients together and work into a smooth dough. Shape into a ball, wrap in cling film and place in the fridge for at least 30 minutes, or until required.

Preheat the oven to 180°C/Gas 4. Line a 28 x 22cm rectangular baking tin with greaseproof paper.

In a clean, dry bowl whisk the egg whites until stiff. In a separate bowl, cream together the butter and sugar. Add the egg yolks and ricotta, mixing well, then gently fold in the whisked egg whites. Set aside.

To make the crumble, place the flour into a bowl, add the chunks of butter and rub between your fingers until it resembles breadcrumbs. Stir in the sugar. Set aside.

Remove the pastry from the fridge and on a lightly floured work surface, roll out to about ½cm thick. Line the baking tin with the pastry and pour over the ricotta mixture. Arrange the peach halves in the mix and top with the crumble.

Bake in the preheated oven for 40–45 minutes until golden. Leave to cool completely, then cut into slices and serve.

2 **eggs**, separated
50g **butter**, softened
125g **sugar**
500g **ricotta**
400g **peaches**, cut into halves and pitted

PASTRY
300g **plain flour**
salt
100g **icing sugar**
1 **egg yolk**
200g **butter**, softened and cut into small pieces
1 tsp finely grated **lemon zest**

CRUMBLE
175g **plain flour**
100g **butter**, cut into small pieces
100g **sugar**

SERVES 6

Carluccio

Torta di Nocciole
HAZELNUT CAKE

Hazelnuts, nocciole *or* avellane, *are grown all over Italy – in the mountains, near the sea, on the plains and often near cities. One such city, Avellino in Campania, actually takes its name from the product for which it is most celebrated. Apart from the hazelnuts of Avellino, I would only use the variety known as* delle Langhe, *which grows in Piedmont. When toasted these nuts exude an unbeatable flavour, and they make delicious cakes, biscuits and sweets.*

Preheat the oven to 180°C/Gas 4. Butter and flour a loose-bottomed 25cm cake tin.

Put the hazelnuts on a baking tray and toast in the oven for about 15 minutes until the flaky skins are loose and the nuts have turned a golden brown. When cool enough, remove as much of the skin as you can. Finely chop the nuts.

In a bowl, beat the butter with 70g of the sugar until smooth. Stir in the egg yolks, the flour and orange rind. In another bowl mix the mascarpone and ricotta and beat until smooth. Mix these two together.

Beat the egg whites in a third bowl with the remaining sugar until stiff. Using a large metal spoon, fold the egg white and the chopped hazelnuts into the butter and cheese mixture.

Pour the cake mixture into the prepared tin and bake in the oven for 25 minutes, or until a skewer inserted in the centre comes out dry. Leave to cool before finishing.

Cut the cake in two horizontally. Spread the bottom half with jam, and put the other half of the cake on top. Melt the chocolate, and drizzle it over the top. Leave to set before serving. This cake is good for morning coffee or afternoon tea, or for dessert, and makes for a very nourishing snack for when the children come home starving from school.

100g **unsalted butter**, softened, plus extra for greasing
150g **hazelnuts**
125g **caster sugar**
4 large **eggs**, separated
30g **plain flour**
2 tbsp grated **orange rind**
50g **mascarpone**
75g **ricotta**
6–7 tbsp **raspberry jelly** or fine jam
30g **dark chocolate**

SERVES 6–8

Chocolate CONTALDO

Most Italian chocolate is made from fine cocoa beans imported from Africa and South America. Chocolate is made throughout Italy, but often in the northern regions as the cooler weather benefits its production. It is said the best chocolates come from Turin, where original methods are still used to create the best possible taste. This is where the famous *gianduiotti* (boat-shaped) chocolates are made, using Piedmont's hazelnuts; and it is where the popular hazelnut spread originates! It is used in cakes and desserts, to cover dried fruit and even, in a traditional southern way, mixed with pig's blood! Powdered drinking chocolate is popular and given to children for *merenda* (snack time).

2 **gelatine leaves**
600ml **double cream**
60g **caster sugar**
1 **vanilla pod**
2 tbsp **dark rum**

SYRUP
2 **limes**
100g **caster sugar**

SERVES 6

Pannacotta con Sciroppo di Lima

BAKED CREAM WITH LIME SYRUP

This dish without doubt has conquered the gastronomic world. One of the main reasons for its popularity is its simplicity, and another is the sheer pleasure of eating it. The recipe's exact origins are not known, but according to the people of the Aosta Valley, it is an echo of the French crème caramel from Savoy– although here it is made with gelatine instead of eggs. The idea of pannacotta as a savoury has been adopted in Piedmont, where it is served with truffle and is called crema cotta *(cooked cream).*

Soak the gelatine leaves in water to cover until soft.

To prepare the limes for the syrup, cut off the zest with a vegetable peeler, avoiding the pith. Squeeze the juice from the limes, then cut the zest into very fine julienne strips. Keep to one side.

In a saucepan, bring the double cream briefly to the boil with sugar, the vanilla pod and rum for just a few seconds. Remove from the heat, then let cool a little. Remove the vanilla pod (this can be dried and used again).

Drain the gelatine, squeezing out excess water, and add to the hot cream. Stir so that the gelatine dissolves completely. Pour the cream into six simple containers, leave to cool, then chill.

To make the syrup, put the sugar, lime juice and julienne zest strips into a small pan, and heat gently. When the sugar is clear the syrup is ready. Leave to cool completely.

Turn the pannacotta out of their containers onto individual serving plates. Pour 1 tablespoon of the syrup over the top of each. Serve.

Editorial Director Jane O'Shea
Creative Director Helen Lewis
Project Editor Simon Davis
Editor Susan Fleming
Editorial Assistant Louise McKeever
Designer Claire Peters
Design Assistant Nicola Davidson
Photographer David Loftus
Food Stylists Georgina Socratous, Anna Jones
Production Director Vincent Smith
Production Controller James Finan

First published in 2012 by
Quadrille Publishing Limited
Alhambra House
27–31 Charing Cross Road
London WC2H 0LS
www.quadrille.co.uk

Reprinted in 2012
10 9 8 7 6 5 4 3 2

Cataloguing in Publication Data: a catalogue record
for this book is available from the British Library.

ISBN 978 184949 109 9

Printed in China

Carluccio

Special thanks have to go to Susan Fleming. If it hadn't been for all her hours of hard work, this book would not have been written. Also to her very understanding husband, Rod, who let me gatecrash their summer holiday at Villa Diana (Lago Maggiore): not many would have put up with me, let alone their wife working most of the holiday. Thank you for doing yet another beautiful job of editing the Two Greedy Italians, much love to you both. To my ever-present assistant, Anna-Louise Naylor-Leyland, who always keeps me on the right track. To David Loftus for the beautiful photography. To my agent Pat White, my publisher Quadrille and those who made the book possible – Alison Cathie, Jane O'Shea, Claire Peters, Simon Davis – and, last but by no means least, Zoe Collins and her amazing team at Fresh One Productions for putting up with the Two Greedy Italians for the second time!

CONTALDO

Thank you to: Liz Przybylski for writing. Adriana Contaldo for testing recipes. David Loftus for gorgeous photography. Susan Fleming and Simon Davis for editing. Jane O'Shea and the rest of the team at Quadrille Publishing. Georgina Socratous for food styling. Paolo Baietti for his recipe tips on northern Italian cuisine. Zoe Collins and her team at Fresh One Productions. My agents Debbie Catchpole and Verity O'Brien. Antonio Carluccio for coming with me again!

And a big thank you to all the people we met on our travels in Italy